Answered Prayer:
The Jesus Plan

by William Ray

PRAISE FOR *ANSWERED PRAYER: THE JESUS PLAN*

Jim Daly, President - Focus on the Family: "Ray has dissected this famous prayer in a way that shows us what it looks like to approach God with adoration, purpose and genuine faith."

Gary Boal, Homiléō, Northern Ireland: "I found myself thrilled by the truths unpacked . . . a glimpse of God through the Biblical revelations that Ray offers . . . a useful tool for study and one that I definitely recommend."

Brian Anderson, Senior Pastor, Vineyard Church of North Phoenix: "A great book. It encouraged me in my prayer life, and I know it will others as well."

Chris Danielson, Real Remnant Radio: "William Ray has hit on something special with this book. The insights are perceptive, yet basic and easy to understand. I would recommend this book to both old and young believers alike. This book will draw you closer to God."

Tama Westman, The Christian Communicator: "A compelling, interesting read . . . clear and powerful."

Answered Prayer: The Jesus Plan

Seaborne Books
Originally published by Ambassador International

ISBN: 9781723977473

Cover design by Detlef Klewer

Dedication

To Mom and Lynette,
whose prayers were answered.

My special thanks to those who've called me "Pastor" over the years, the people of Desert Joy Christian Fellowship, West Glendale Baptist Church, and Traders Village Christian Fellowship. It was an honor to serve among you—and witness so many answers to prayer.

CONTENTS

Chapter 1:

JESUS AND THE MYSTERY OF PRAYER

ON THE MORNING OF SEPTEMBER 11, 2001, Stanley Praimnath was riding in the elevator of the south tower of the World Trade Center when American Airlines Flight 11 struck the north tower. Being in the elevator, he had not heard the explosion from the north tower. But when Stanley walked into his office on the 81st floor (he was an assistant vice president at Fuji Bank), he saw a red-orange flame coming from the north tower.

With others, he went back down the elevator. But in the lobby loudspeakers assured everyone that their building was secure; they could return to their offices. With others, Stanley got back on the elevator.

He was back at his desk, on the phone, when a giant airplane caught his eye out the window. He heard its engines rev as it grew bigger and bigger, coming head-on. He dove under his desk—on top of which he always kept a Bible—and he said a prayer: "Lord, I can't do this. You take over."

The nose of United Airlines Flight 175 crashed into Stanley's very floor; a "wing," he said, "sliced right through the office." There was a deafening explosion (Stanley would suffer temporary hearing loss), a ball of flame, and then darkness.

Stanley was the only one left on the 81st floor. In fact, upon impact everyone on floors 78-82 had been swept away. Stanley at first thought they had heartlessly left

1

him behind, before he realized later what had happened. The ceiling was caved in, part of the floor collapsed, partitions and walls flattened, and every piece of furniture and all computers destroyed. Everything except for Stanley's desk, under which he huddled, somehow alive.

The documentary that told Stanley's story (*Miracles in Our Midst*) pointed out that with the epicenter of the crash less than fifty yards from Stanley's desk, and thousands of gallons of jet fuel igniting,

"the banker's chances of survival should be nonexistent. Yet when the cataclysmic roar of the crash subsided, Stanley Praimnath is very much alive."

Stanley, after more answers to prayer, made it out of the building.

He said, "There is a God, and He hears and intervenes."

Stanley Praimnath credited his miraculous escape to a prayer.

THE MYSTERY OF PRAYER

As a former atheist who had an experience with God through a simple, heart-felt prayer, I understandably have been fascinated by prayer ever since. In that moment twenty-five years ago, I became aware, quite suddenly and surprisingly, of the supernatural power of prayer.

In my years as a pastor, I've had the privilege of seeing many prayers get answered—prayers of individuals, prayers by congregations, and a fair number of my own prayers. Prayer is exciting.

It is also mysterious.

First of all, sometimes prayers don't get answered. For example, I am sure that many other prayers on 9/11 went unanswered, even as Stanley Praimnath was escaping. Why is it that some prayers don't get answered?

Second, even though I know prayer is the Great Invitation—to talk to Almighty God, King of the Universe—sometimes I'm not motivated to do it. Why is that?

Third, there are many different approaches to prayer, so much so that it can be confusing. For example, in an ad in my local paper, a New Age group said the thing to do is find a quiet place and sing the sound HU (pronounced "hue") as a song of love. For some, the time of day and the posture of prayer are important. We're all familiar with television images of devout Muslims kneeling in prayer together. For others, the place is important. We're all familiar with television images of devout Jews who practice prayer at the "Wailing Wall." In the religion I grew up in, the number of prayers was important. To be forgiven for our sins, we were instructed to pray specific memorized prayers a certain number of times.

And there are various other approaches to prayer—from lighting candles, to wearing certain articles of clothing, to meditation. I even came across a uniquely modern approach to prayer: a website that offered to send your prayers via radio wave transmitter to the place in the universe where the Big Bang may have occurred, and which was, therefore—according to the website— "the last known location of GOD."

Which of these approaches is right?

WHO HAS THE ANSWERS?

Who should we listen to when it comes to the mystery of prayer?

My choice is Jesus Christ. According to the pages of the New Testament, Jesus had insight into prayer that no one else has ever had. In the Gospel of John, He prayed, *"Father, I thank you that you have heard me. **I knew that you always hear me,** but I said this for the benefit of the people standing here, that they may believe that you sent me"* (John 11:41b-42, emphasis added). Jesus said that He knew God always heard His prayers, which was another way of saying that God always answered His prayers. Who else could make such a claim? Jesus did— and then backed it up by raising Lazarus from the dead in response to His prayer (John 11:43-44)!

In the next chapter of the Gospel of John, Jesus prayed spontaneously, *"Father, glorify your name!"* The Bible says that a voice came from heaven: *"I have glorified it, and will glorify it again."* God was carrying on an *out loud* conversation with Jesus from heaven. (The people were so shocked that some said that the voice from heaven must have been thunder.) It is impressive enough that God would carry on an out-loud conversation with Jesus from heaven, but it is perhaps even more impressive that this did not impress Jesus! He said to the bystanders, *"This voice was for your benefit, not mine."* Prayer was so real to Jesus, silent or otherwise, that He did not need to hear the sound of God's audible voice to make it more real (John 12:28-30).

Not to mention the fact that He walked on water, calmed storms, and healed all kinds of sicknesses and disabilities—all of which, He said, came from His prayer

4

relationship with the Heavenly Father: *"I tell you the truth, the Son can do nothing by Himself; He can do only what He sees His Father doing, because whatever the Father does the Son also does"* (John 5:19). If Jesus *saw* what the Father was doing, that means He was in communication with Him. Communication with God is another name for prayer.

The same is true of His teaching, which has changed the world—He said he got it from His prayer relationship with the Father: *Jesus answered, "My teaching is not my own. It comes from him who sent me"* (John 7:16).

Who should we listen to when it comes to the mystery of prayer? I think the answer is Jesus Christ.

THE MODEL PRAYER

The good news is, Jesus taught us what He knew! He taught about prayer in many places in the Bible, but especially in the Lord's Prayer—or, as it is often called, the Model Prayer.

> *This, then, is how you should pray:*

> *"Our Father in heaven, hallowed be Your name,*
> *Your kingdom come, Your will be done on earth as it is in heaven.*
> *Give us today our daily bread.*
> *Forgive us our debts, as we also have forgiven our debtors.*
> *And lead us not into temptation, but deliver us from the evil one,*
> *for Yours is the kingdom and the power and the*

5

glory forever. Amen." (Matt. 6:9-13)

I prefer "Model Prayer" to "Lord's Prayer" as a name for this prayer for two reasons. First, this prayer contains a line that Jesus Himself could never have prayed: *"Forgive us our debts"* (12). The Bible is clear that Jesus was sinless (1 Pet. 2:22, Heb. 4:15), so He could never have personally prayed this prayer.

Second, this prayer was meant to be just that: a *model* for prayer. Sometimes Christians pray this prayer word for word. There is nothing wrong with that, especially in group situations, like in church. But if the repetition of this prayer becomes an empty ritual, just words we repeat over and over because we think they will earn us favor with God, then we are violating Jesus' own words in His introduction to the Model Prayer: *"And when you pray, do not keep on babbling like pagans, for they think they will be heard because of their many words"* (Matt. 6:7). Jesus gave this prayer to us as a model—to show us the kinds of things we should pray about, and how we should pray about them.

THE KEY TO UNDERSTANDING THE MODEL PRAYER

I was on my way to give a member of our church a ride to prayer meeting. As I drove, I was thinking about verse 10 of the Model Prayer: *"Your kingdom come, your will be done on earth as it is in heaven."* (A practice of mine, since early in my Christian life, has been to pick a verse of Scripture, run it through my mind and heart, and ask the Lord, "What does this verse mean to me? How does it change my life?" This is meditating on the

Scriptures.) As I thought about this verse, it dawned on me: *Jesus would not have told me to pray a prayer that didn't work. Therefore, when I ask for His kingdom to come, it must come in some form or fashion.*

Well, that was an exciting thought! I couldn't wait to get back to the prayer meeting and start praying for His *kingdom to come* in some areas!

I felt like that thought had come from the Lord Himself, and I realized that it must be true for every line of the Model Prayer. *If Jesus told us to pray it, it must be because it will work.* As I began to look at the Model Prayer with this truth in mind, I began to see it in a whole new light: as the basis—or springboard—for a *real*, exciting relationship with God.

Understanding that Jesus would not have told us to pray a prayer that didn't work is the key to understanding the Model Prayer. It means that everything He told us to pray in the Model Prayer will bring results; it will result in real communication with God, real answers—a real relationship.

In the coming chapters, we'll look line by line at the Model Prayer. We'll see how each line of the prayer was meant to bring about *answered* prayer, and a personal experience with God.

But we'll start with the verses that introduce the prayer, because they contain one of the most exciting promises in Scripture.

Chapter 2

HAVING A RELATIONSHIP WITH GOD THROUGH PRAYER

IF YOU COULD ASK JESUS to teach you how to do one thing, what would it be? It would be an exciting opportunity, since He knows everything. You could ask Him how to pick the right stocks or how to get the job you always wanted. You could ask Him how to be a great athlete or how to get so-and-so to fall in love with you. You could ask Him to show you how to find the cure for cancer, how to have the greatest marriage, or how to raise kids right. It would be a great opportunity to be able to ask the Lord to teach you one thing.

The disciples had this opportunity when they walked the earth with Jesus. They saw Him perform great miracles, but there's no record that they ever asked Him how they could perform miracles. They heard Him teach life-changing truths, but there's no record that they ever asked Him the secret to being a great teacher. They saw Him attract huge crowds, but there's no record that they ever asked Him the key to building a big following.

What did the disciples ask Jesus to teach them? In Luke 11:1, they asked Him, "Lord, teach us to pray." Out of all the things they could have asked Jesus to teach them, they asked Him to teach them to pray. Why? Because they had seen in His prayer life the most exciting thing in the world: a real relationship with God. In fact, their request to teach them to pray came right after hearing Him pray:

One day Jesus was praying in a certain place. When He finished, one of His disciples said to Him, "Lord, teach us to pray" (Luke 11:1).

They heard in His prayer life a real relationship with God, and there was nothing more exciting.

In His introduction to the Model Prayer, the verses preceding the actual prayer, Jesus taught that we can all have a real relationship with God through prayer:

> *And when you pray, do not be like the hypocrites, for they love to pray standing in the synagogues and on the street corners to be seen by others. Truly I tell you, they have received their reward in full. But when you pray, go into your room, close the door and pray to your Father, who is unseen. Then your Father, who sees what is done in secret, will reward you. And when you pray, do not keep on babbling like pagans, for they think they will be heard because of their many words. Do not be like them, for your Father knows what you need before you ask Him* (Matt. 6:5-8).

In verse 6 Jesus said, "But when you pray, go into your room, close the door and pray to your Father, who is unseen. Then your Father, who sees what is done in secret, will reward you." This is one of the most remarkable statements in the Bible. Jesus says that when we go to prayer, Almighty God Himself responds:

- He "sees what is done in secret" (our act of going to prayer).
- He will "reward you" (for going to prayer).

This is amazing if we take it seriously (and remember, that's the key to understanding the Model Prayer, realizing that Jesus would not have told us to engage in prayer that didn't work). Almighty God, who has the whole universe to run, responds when you go to prayer. He notices what you're doing, and He even *rewards* it. The point is, Almighty God is responding to you. There's a real *relationship* happening here!

It's exciting, isn't it?

THREE REQUIREMENTS

In these verses introducing the Model Prayer, Jesus lists three requirements we must meet if we want to have a real relationship with God through prayer.

The first requirement is desire. We must desire a relationship with God more than we desire the approval of other people.

And when you pray, do not be like the hypocrites, for they love to pray standing in the synagogues and on the street corners to be seen by others. Truly I tell you, they have received their reward in full (Matt. 6:5).

Jesus said some people pray only to look good to others. In His day they did this in the "synagogues," the first century version of the local church, and on "street corners." He called them "hypocrites." In the Greek, the language of the New Testament, the word is *hupokrites,* and in Jesus' day it literally meant an actor. Greek and Roman actors wore large masks when they performed a play. The masks had built-in mechanical devices for magnifying the voice. Jesus was saying that people who prayed only to impress others were like actors wearing masks and using false voices. They wanted to look good to others, to seem spiritual, but they really didn't have a prayer relationship with God. And looking good to others, Jesus said, would be their only reward. They would receive nothing from God.

There's nothing wrong with praying in public. Jesus, the apostles, and the prophets all did it. It's only wrong if our *motivation* is "to be seen by men," (Matt. 6:5) or if praying in public is the only place we pray.

To have a relationship with God through prayer we must desire it—and we must desire it for its own sake, not to impress others. How would a husband feel if the only time his wife showed him affection and paid him attention was in public or at family gatherings, while at home she had nothing to do with him? He would feel that she didn't really love him, that her actions were just a show. I imagine God feels the same way if we don't have time for Him except in public.

The first requirement for a real relationship with God through prayer is desire.

The second requirement is a meeting place.

But when you pray, go into your room, close the door and pray to your Father, who is unseen. Then your Father, who sees what is done in secret, will reward you (Matt. 6:6).

We need to have a place we can meet privately—even secretly—with
God. Jesus did. *"Very early in the morning, while it was still dark, Jesus got up, left the house and went off*

11

to a solitary place, where He prayed" (Mark 1:35). He met privately with God first thing in the morning. This was his top priority.

After feeding the five thousand with the five loaves and two fish, He sent the crowd away and *"went up on a mountainside by Himself to pray. When evening came, He was there alone"* (Matt. 14:23b). He sent the crowd away, then He went and met with His Father. It was more important to Him to be alone with God than with an adoring crowd. Why does our meeting place with God need to be private? So we can be sure we're praying for God's eyes only, that our motivation is just to be with Him. If we "publicize" our prayer life, our motivation might be to look spiritual to others. But if we're praying for God's eyes only, God knows.

And Jesus said that Almighty God will respond to this! He will "reward" us. Would you like to receive a "reward" from God today? Jesus has told you exactly what to do.

How will God reward us for meeting with Him? One reward is some peace and quiet. People's lives today are often too busy and crowded. You might say that they lack margin. Margin on a page, of course, is the empty space around the text. Margin in our lives is some space to breathe. We tend to run from one activity to another, one meeting to another, and are always connected—by cell phones, email, text messages, Facebook, the Internet, laptops, and iPads, etc. Some private time in a meeting place with God will help build some margin in our life, and help us remember what is really important.

Another reward for meeting with God—perhaps the main reward Jesus was referring to—is answered prayer. If we meet with God for His eyes only, He will gladly do

12

things for us.

I used to get my hair cut in an old-fashioned barbershop. A TV in the corner played daytime programs. Magazines were strewn here and there on empty chairs. Hair clippings gathered on the floor. The barber was a hard-working entrepreneur who had moved to the Phoenix area from Chicago. He knew I was a pastor. One day, when no one else was in the shop, he opened up and told me why he believed in prayer.

His unit got caught in a rice paddy in Vietnam. For weeks they were hemmed in and couldn't get out, and they were in constant danger from enemy fire. They were eaten by leeches. Finally, a helicopter rescued them.

It was a miserable time, and the barber freely admitted that combat was not for him. So back in camp, while his friends were out "whoring and drinking," as he put it, he went to chapel and prayed to be spared any more combat action. While his friends were out partying, he went and met with God about the desire of his heart.

Not long after offering his prayer, he found his path crossing an officer's. Before he knew what he was saying, he found himself asking,

"Sir, you need a barber?" He told me he didn't know why he said it—he hadn't thought of it the moment before.

The officer stopped in his tracks. "You a stateside barber?" he asked. "Licensed?"

"Yes, sir."

The officer placed a call to a general, who had just lost his regular barber. The officer asked if he'd like a new one. And with that my barber became the general's barber. He never had to return to combat. When he was leaving Vietnam, he inquired about his old unit and was

13

told, "They were all killed." The barber told me he wasn't a religious man, and it wasn't until years later that it dawned on him that God had answered that prayer in the chapel and saved his life.

The main reward of a meeting place with God is answered prayer.

We've seen so far that the first requirement for a real relationship with God through prayer is desire, and the second requirement is a meeting place.

The third requirement is trust that He hears us.

And when you pray, do not keep on babbling like pagans, for they think they will be heard because of their many words. Do not be like them, for your Father knows what you need before you ask Him (Matt. 6:7-8).

Jesus said we don't have to use "many words" (7) to be heard in prayer; we don't have to earn a hearing by how long we pray, how loud we pray, or how hard we pray. Jesus said our Heavenly Father knows what we need before we ask Him. Jesus is telling us we can trust that God hears the prayers of our heart.

The third requirement for a real prayer relationship with God is to trust that He hears us. Trust is a necessity for every relationship. Do you draw close to people you don't trust? No, you stay away from them. Trust is a necessity for a relationship. To have a real relationship with God through prayer, we must trust that He hears us.

One thing that will help us trust that God hears us is to remember that He has more than one way to answer a prayer. Many have lost confidence in prayer because they asked for something and didn't get it. They've

14

concluded that prayer must not work, at least for them. They have failed to understand that God, like any good parent, has more than one answer to a request. Usually when we talk about answers to prayer, we're talking about the "Yes" answer—when we get what we want. But that's just one answer, though admittedly the most popular one. God has at least *four different answers to prayer:*

1. "No" is one answer to prayer.

Sometimes we're asking for something that is not God's will for us. What we want may be bad for us down the road, or it may deflect us from God's ultimate plan for us. As parents, don't we tell our children "No" sometimes? Don't we shake our heads at parents who don't seem to have this ability with their children, and end up spoiling them? Certainly our perfect Heavenly Father is sometimes going to say "No" to His children's requests.

2. "Slow," as in "slow down," is another answer to prayer.

Sometimes the *timing* is not right. It's God's will to give us what we're asking for, but not yet. He is going to answer the prayer, but on His timetable, not ours. We need to "slow down" and wait.

3. "Grow," as in "grow up spiritually," is another answer to prayer.

Sometimes the Lord has to wait for us to mature before He can give us what He wants to give us. We're not ready yet. We've all heard stories of lottery winners who end up broke and broken. They weren't ready to handle all that money.

God, on the other hand, likes for His children to *grow* into their blessings and responsibilities. He's generally a rather slow promoter. Joseph, though innocent, spent years in prison before God elevated him to his place of responsibility and authority in Egypt. Moses spent forty years in the desert before God deemed he was ready for his great calling. The apostles spent three years on the road with Jesus before being released into their ministry.

God wants us to grow into our blessings, so that we will have the ability to handle them well. Therefore, sometimes His answer to prayer is "Grow."

4. "Go," as in "Yes, it's a go!" is the fourth answer to prayer.*

When the *request* is right (it's God's will), the *timing* is right (it's God's time), and we're right (we've matured enough to handle what *we're* asking for), God says, "Yes," to our prayer!

"Yes" is our favorite answer, but we need to remember that all the answers are good for us. He has heard us whatever the answer. We must trust this to have a real prayer relationship with God.

A REAL RELATIONSHIP

According to Jesus, each one of us has the incredible ability to *move* Almighty God. It doesn't take some superhuman effort. You don't have to be one of a few select holy men. You don't have to be a theologian. All you have to do is take the simple step Jesus said to take: "Go into your room, close the door and pray to your Father, who is unseen. Then your Father, who sees what

16

is done in secret, will reward you" (Matt. 6:6). God Himself will respond to you; He will notice and He will reward!

Can you think of anything more exciting than that? Your Heavenly Father is waiting for you.

SUMMARY

The disciples asked Jesus to teach them to pray because they saw in His prayer life the most exciting thing in the world: a real relationship with God. In the introduction to the Model Prayer, Jesus taught that we can all have such a relationship, that God Himself *responds* when we take the time to meet with Him in prayer—He *sees* us, He *rewards* us. Jesus listed three requirements necessary for such a relationship: the desire for the relationship, a meeting place, and trust that God hears us.

DIGGING DEEPER

Let's dig a little deeper now and see what some other Bible passages have to say about the reality of having a relationship with God through prayer. We'll look at what the Scriptures say, then consider how it applies to our personal lives. There will be a place to record your answers; below that I will give my suggested answers.

If you prefer to continue reading specifically about the Model Prayer, you can turn to Chapter 3 now and return here later to dig a little deeper.

BAD NEWS? (FROM ISAIAH 38:1-22)

How do you react when you receive bad news? A wrong reaction, I'm sure you've noticed, can make matters worse.

Mrs. Monroe of Darlington, Maryland, learned what can happen when we make the wrong move when confronted with bad news or difficult circumstances. This mother of eight came home from the grocery store one afternoon to find five of her children in the living room playing with skunks! These skunks had somehow found their way into her house—bad news indeed. Things might have turned out okay if Mrs. Monroe had kept her cool and calmly directed the children to lead the skunks back outdoors. Instead, she panicked and screamed, and that was her mistake. She scared the kids and the skunks—and you know what skunks do when they're afraid!

Our reaction to bad news and difficult circumstances can make all the difference. How do you react when you receive bad news? King Hezekiah of Judah received some bad news. He was deathly ill when the prophet Isaiah came to him, and Isaiah's message was not what Hezekiah wanted to hear:

"This is what the LORD says: Put your house in order, because you are going to die; you will not recover" (Isa. 38:1b).

This was the height of bad news: being told he was going to die. And it wasn't news that came from a doctor, lab technician, or any other human, but from God Himself. It was very bad news.

Hezekiah's reaction to this news saved his life. As the prophet left his room, the Bible says, *"Hezekiah turned*

his face to the wall and prayed to the LORD" (Isa. 38:2).
Here's what he prayed:

"Remember, O LORD, how I have walked before you faithfully and with wholehearted devotion and have done what is good in your eyes." And Hezekiah wept bitterly (Isa. 38:3).

What happened? God sent Isaiah to Hezekiah again, this time with a better message:

"Go and tell Hezekiah, 'This is what the LORD, the God of your father David, says: I have heard your prayer and seen your tears; I will add fifteen years to your life. And I will deliver you and this city from the hand of the king of Assyria. I will defend this city (Isa. 38:5-6).

God promised Hezekiah more years, and He promised to protect Jerusalem from the enemies that threatened her.

God's word came true. Hezekiah was healed. Isaiah told the attendants to *"Prepare a poultice of figs and apply it to the boil, and he will recover"* (Isa. 38:21b), and this application of natural medicine brought about Hezekiah's healing (which, by the way, is evidence that doctors and the medical profession are God's partners in His healing work).

And Jerusalem was spared invasion in Hezekiah's lifetime.

What brought about these wonderful answers to prayer? I believe the key is found in the words, "Hezekiah turned his face to the wall" (Isa. 38:2a). By turning his face to the wall before he prayed, Hezekiah was indicating that he was looking to God for help. He was beyond the help of people. Being king was not going to help him out of this problem. It was God or no one. That wall became a *meeting place* with God for Hezekiah. God saw and responded.

When bad news strikes, how do you respond? Think about a recent occasion when bad news came to you— when tough times popped up. How did you respond?

The difficult circumstance: _____

Your response: _____

Based on what you've learned from Hezekiah's experience, how should you have responded?

_____

_____

_____

(It's not wrong, of course, to turn to other people for help when problems occur, or to make use of the resources and blessings we have at our disposal. But we often make things worse—or at least not any better— because we forget our greatest resource when bad news strikes: our Heavenly Father. Turn to Him and see what He does.)

ONE THING NEEDED (FROM LUKE 10:38-42)

Once when Jesus was traveling, He was welcomed into the home of a couple of sisters named Martha and Mary. These sisters were exact opposites. Martha was a go-getter. As soon as Jesus entered her home, she got busy getting things ready. You can imagine how she felt. After all, the biggest celebrity in the nation was in her home, along with His entourage. There were refreshments to get, rooms to straighten, towels to put out—or whatever first century Holy Land hospitality required. The Bible says she *"was distracted by all the preparations that had to be made"* (Luke 10:40a).

Her sister Mary had a different response to Jesus' visit. She didn't help Martha get anything ready. She didn't worry about making the house respectable for the neighbors who were dropping in to check out this traveling miracle worker. She didn't offer to run next door to borrow some extra bread. What did Mary do? The Bible says she *"sat at the Lord's feet listening to what He said"* (Luke 10:39b). She just sat there in Jesus' presence while her sister Martha did all the work.

Well, you can imagine how Martha felt about the third or fourth time she brought in a plate from the kitchen— and there was Mary just sitting there like one of the guests. Finally, it was too much, and she said to Jesus, *"Lord, don't you care that my sister has left me to do the work by myself? Tell her to help me!"* (Luke 10:40b).

How do you think Jesus responded to Martha's complaint? Do you think He sympathized with her? Maybe said something like, "You're right. Mary, you should get up and help your sister do the work"? His answer might surprise you:

"Martha, Martha," the Lord answered, "You are worried and upset about many things, but few things are needed—or indeed only one. Mary has chosen what is better, and it will not be taken away from her" (Luke 10:41-42).

Jesus did not rebuke Mary. Rather, He commended

her for choosing to sit before Him and listen to His teaching. He even said that her choice was the "one" thing needed" in life.

What can He mean here, because He's certainly aware of all the necessities of life pressing in on us—work, financial issues, health concerns, family and relationship responsibilities, and so on? What can He mean that, in spite of all these concerns, the one thing needed is to spend time with Him? He means that time with Him is the key to handling all of the concerns of life successfully. He means that if we will spend time with Him, God Himself will see to it that everything else works out. In other words, time with God is the most practical thing we can do:

- It gives us peace, which leads to wise decisions.
- It gives us direction—as we listen to Jesus' words in the Bible.
- It gives us real help from God.

And it's help we need. Several years ago, *USA Today* asked experts from various fields to estimate how much time was needed for the daily necessities of life—how much time was needed per day to exercise properly, to brush our teeth, to play with the kids, to drive to work, to get a good night's sleep, and so forth. When all the estimates from all the experts were added up, the time needed for the daily necessities of life came to forty-two hours a day! In other words, there literally are not enough hours in the day to do everything the experts want you to do. You may feel that way about your own life: overwhelmed with all you face. That's why meeting with God is the most practical step you can take. God can do more by moving His little finger than you and I can with a lifetime of effort. That's why Jesus says the one thing needed is to come to Him. It will give us real help from God. He will see to it that everything else falls into place.

What are some things that compete for the "one thing needed" spot in your life?

_____

_____

How might these areas of your life improve if you spent time with Jesus first?

_____

_____

What's one thing you haven't been able to change by your own effort, which perhaps God will change for you as you spend time with Him?

_____

_____

PATIENCE (FROM DANIEL 10)

Americans aren't big on patience. We've grown used to getting things fast and easy. An article in my local paper chronicled how we've become used to getting things quicker and quicker. For example:

- We used to have to wait days to get our pictures. Then there was One-Hour Photo. Now there's instant digital.
- We used to have to spend some time in the sun to get a tan. Then came tanning salons. Now there are spray-on tans.
- The average news story is only four sentences.
- In European history there was such a thing as the

Hundred Years War. When the latest War in Iraq had gone longer than a week, TV pundits were already wondering what had gone wrong.

- In 1893, Cream of Wheat took fifteen minutes to prepare, and it was considered a fast breakfast for the time. By 1939, Cream of Wheat was down to five minutes to prepare. Today it's down to thirty seconds.
- Even the old-fashioned world of classical music has changed. In Beethoven's time, a classical music concert could last six hours. Even fifteen years ago, the standard concert was two hours long. Today's music lovers get restless if a program exceeds ninety minutes.

We have grown accustomed to instant cash from ATMs, microwave ovens, overnight delivery from across the country, fast cars, fast planes, fast computers, broadband Internet, and drive-through everything— from restaurants to banks to drugstores to Starbucks. Patience is not our strong suit. We like things fast and easy.

Yet there are going to be times when we need to have patience, even in our modern society. A *Chicago Tribune* article estimated that the amount of time spent sitting at stoplights in a lifetime was six months! And the Texas Transportation Institute said the average American will spend about fifty hours per year in gridlock—trapped in traffic, bumper to bumper. We still need patience in our modern world.

And then there are those life moments when nothing will do but a patient sigh. A first grade teacher had such a moment when she had finished helping her thirty-two students put on their galoshes. The last little girl said,

"You know what, teacher? These aren't my galoshes."
The teacher paused a moment, then removed one galosh
and then the other from the girl's feet. The girl said,
"They're my sisters, and she lets me wear them." The
teacher paused another moment, breathed deeply, and
put the galoshes back on the girl's feet.

We may not be big on it, but there are times when
patience is a necessity.

That is true when it comes to prayer, too. We have
seen in this chapter that God promises to see and reward
us when we come to a *meeting place* with Him in prayer,
and that one of those rewards is answered prayer. God
promised the reward would come, but He didn't promise
when it would appear. It may appear immediately, it may
appear a few days or weeks later, or it may appear much
later. When the answer is delayed, we have a need for
patience.

One of the things that will help us wait patiently is to
realize that though the answer may not have appeared
yet, it's already been sent. We see this remarkable truth
in a story from the prophet Daniel's life. Daniel was one
of the Israelites taken to Babylon by King
Nebuchadnezzar when he attacked and eventually
overthrew Judah and Jerusalem. After being in exile a
long time, Daniel began to pray for the return of his
people to Jerusalem and for the future of his fallen
nation. One day he had a vision and a heavenly
messenger appeared to him and said:

*"Do not be afraid, Daniel. **Since the first day** that you
set your mind to gain understanding and to humble
yourself before your God, your words were heard, and I
have come in response to them"* (Dan. 10:12b, emphasis

25

added).

Notice that the heavenly messenger (who seems to be the angel Gabriel) told Daniel that his words of prayer had been heard "*Since the first day* . . . and I have come in response to them." God had heard Daniel's prayer and sent the answer from the moment Daniel prayed, but the angel was only now arriving with the answer (and it was twenty-three days later, as we'll see in a moment).

Isn't that an encouraging truth? Perhaps you've presented a request to God, and nothing has happened. The truth is, nothing you've *seen* has happened. An answer, perhaps in the person of an angel, has been sent.

Why the delay then? One possible reason is spiritual warfare. Look at the reason Gabriel gave Daniel for his delay:

"But the prince of the Persian kingdom resisted me twenty-one days. Then Michael, one of the chief princes, came to help me, because I was detained there with the king of Persia" (Dan. 10:13).

Gabriel wasn't delayed by a human prince. The prince he ran into was in the spiritual realm, some kind of evil spirit who was seeking to exert influence in the "Persian kingdom" to hinder the return of the Jews to their land. Gabriel, the messenger angel (remember, he was the one who came with the news of Jesus' birth to Mary), had to have help from "Michael," the warrior angel, to get through this demonic force. There was no doubt that he would get through, for he had been sent by God, but it did take time for him to get through, and help from Michael. Spiritual warfare delayed the answer to Daniel.

You might wonder how demons could possibly put up a meaningful fight against the angels of Almighty God. It's not because demons are anywhere near as strong, but it's because God allows demons to work in a region or situation where people are in agreement with them, whether they know it or not. God gave the earth to men—as I'll discuss in detail in Chapter 4—and He's never taken it back. Generally speaking, He requires our agreement to work in the world; that's the purpose of prayer.

Spiritual warfare may have delayed the answer to your prayer. If so, it's not that there's any doubt the answer will come. It's just that there's a spiritual process that has to be worked out first—things in the background, which perhaps you know nothing about, that have to be cleared up.

So if you've met with God, and feel certain that what you've asked for is according to His will, but you've yet to see any results—be patient. You were heard from the moment you prayed, and the answer was sent.

It just hasn't appeared yet.

What request have you made to God that you're still waiting on?

_____

_____

Do you feel like this is a situation where the delay might be due to spiritual warfare?

_____

_____

If not spiritual warfare, what might be another reason

27

for the delay?

_____

_____

THE FIRST QUESTION (FROM GENESIS 3:1-24)

What question does God ask Adam in the following verses?

Then the man and his wife heard the sound of the LORD God as he was walking in the garden in the cool of the day, and they hid from the LORD God among the trees of the garden. But the LORD God called to the man, "Where are you?" (Gen. 3:8-9).

God asked Adam: _____

("Where are you?")

This is the first recorded question that God ever asked a human being: "Where are you?" God asked this question right after Adam and Eve's sin. In shame, they were hiding from Him behind the trees in the garden. What I want you to notice is that Adam and Eve recognized "the sound of the LORD God as He was walking in the garden" that day. Why? Because they were used to hearing it. It was God's custom to come and visit with them "in the cool of the day."

God's desire from the beginning has been for a relationship with us. We can have that relationship today through prayer. We can have a meeting place with God. The first recorded question God asked a human is the question He still asks us today: "Where are you?"

* The breakdown of the four different ways that God answers prayers isn't mine. I would like to give credit to whoever first came up with it, but I don't know who it was. I heard it "accidentally" years ago through a phone line that was picking up a sermon that was being broadcast on a Christian radio station! I couldn't even tell you the radio station. I think it was a God thing.

My thanks to the original author.

Chapter 3

WORSHIPING GOD THROUGH PRAYER

FLORENCE CHADWICK WAS THE FIRST woman to swim the English Channel in both directions. On July 4, 1952, she set out to accomplish another goal: to be the first woman to swim twenty-one miles from Catalina Island to the California coast. She set out in the morning, battling fatigue and the numbing cold of the water. And there was another problem that day—fog.

Fifteen hours later, Florence signaled to the boats attending her, and asked to be taken out of the water. Her mother and trainer, who were in the boats, urged her to keep going, saying the coast was close. But all Florence could see was the fog, and insisted on quitting. When she was taken out, she discovered that she had been only one half mile from her destination! She declared that she would have kept going if she could have seen the shore.

Her experience reveals a truth: when we lose our vision, we lose our way. When a couple loses hope for their marriage, divorce is on the way. When a young person doesn't have a dream to pursue, he or she is more likely to end up using illegal drugs. When a pastor forgets the privilege of his call, he resigns his church. When we lose our vision, we lose our way. The Bible puts it this way:

Where there is no vision, the people perish (Prov. 29:18a, KJV).

30

One way to keep our vision in life is to be a worshiper of God. When our eyes are on Him, everything else tends to fall into place.

And one way to be a worshiper of God, as Jesus taught in the Model Prayer, is in our prayer life:

This, then, is how you should pray:
"Our Father in heaven, hallowed be Your name" (Matt. 6:9).

Notice that there is no request in this first verse of the Model Prayer. God is not asked to do anything or give anything or help in any way. The verses that follow in the rest of the prayer contain requests:

- "Your kingdom come, Your will be done" (10)
- "Give us today our daily bread" (11)
- "Forgive us" (12)
- "And lead us" (13)
- "deliver us" (13)

But there is no request in the first verse. God is simply addressed intimately (*"Our Father in heaven"*) and reverently ("hallowed be Your name"). The point is, this is a prayer of worship—nothing else.

Jesus' plan for knowing God through prayer starts with worship. Let's answer three questions about worshiping God through prayer: **What does it mean to worship? How do I worship God through prayer? What will it do for me?**

What does it mean to worship?

Worship, simply put, is the act of acknowledging God's worth. Our modern English word "worship" was

31

originally the Old English word "*worth*ship." It means to express *worth*. Because God's worth is eternal, our worship of Him will never end.

Jesus said there are two aspects of God's worth that we should acknowledge as we begin our prayer with worship. *The first is God's Fatherhood.* Jesus told us to start our prayer with the words, "Our *Father* in heaven" (emphasis added). We are worshiping God when we acknowledge Him as our Heavenly Father.

Do you trust God as your Father? You should if you're a Christian, because Galatians 3:26 says, "You are all sons of God through faith in Christ Jesus" (NASB). If you're a believer in Jesus, you are a son or daughter of God. He's your very own Father! And He wants you to trust in Him as the loving Father He is. That's a part of worshiping Him.

Our church had a party for nursery workers at a local park one

Saturday afternoon. I was sitting on the grass watching the children play on the monkey bars. One little toddler named Mia was having a great time. She would hang onto the crossbars with all her might, her face turning red, the ground a couple or three feet beneath her—a *long* way to someone her size. She would hang there as long as she could, then let go and squeal with delight as her dad, grandpa, and mom took turns catching her. Then she wanted to do it again.

And again.

And again.

Here's what caught my attention. Her dad, grandpa, and mom were standing *behind* little Mia. She couldn't see them as she let go and fell through the air. But she never doubted that they would catch her. That was the fun of it. She was letting go. She was falling through the air, but she knew someone bigger and stronger than her was going to catch her. That's how our Heavenly Father wants us to trust Him when it comes to life. He wants us to let go—let go of our burdens and fears and worries—and trust Him to catch us safely. That's worship to Him. It's acknowledging His worth as our Father.

Another aspect of God's worth that we should acknowledge as we begin our prayer with worship is His holiness. Jesus told us to pray, "Our Father in heaven, *hallowed* be Your name" (emphasis added). To hallow something means to set it apart as deserving special honor, as when President Abraham Lincoln spoke of the hallowed ground of Gettysburg. To hallow God's name, then, is to set it apart as holy—above all other names.

Yes, we should trust God as our loving Heavenly Father, but we should always keep in mind that He is Almighty God, too.

There's an amazing scene in the Book of Revelation that describes "four living creatures" who worship God in heaven at His throne. These are unique creatures, "covered with eyes all around." Each one has eyes "in front and in back" and "even under his wings." And the Bible says:

Day and night they never stop saying: "Holy, holy, holy is the Lord God Almighty, who was, and is, and is to come" (Rev. 4:8b).

Here's what I want to notice: though these creatures never leave God's throne (that is, they are close to Him at all times), and though they have eyes all over (that is, they see *everything*), they never stop declaring how holy—how morally perfect, pure, and good—He is! Amazing.

We should trust God as our loving Heavenly Father, but we should acknowledge His holiness as well, realizing that it is only because of His mercy that we are able to approach Him. Keeping both these truths in mind—God's love and His holiness—keeps us balanced.

The story is told of some mountain climbers in the Alps. While two of the climbers were experienced, one was making his first climb in the Alps. They climbed up the rock and snow, and when they reached the summit, the two experienced climbers moved aside to let their friend go first. The young man ascended the summit and was about to jump to his feet—when his two friends pulled him down! When he asked them what they were doing, one of them said, "Hold your hand up." He did and felt a powerful gust of wind.

"Up here," the experienced climber explained, "the only safe place is on your knees."

It is the same with God. We should trust Him as our loving Heavenly Father, but we should also show Him reverence and awe as the Most High. We are worshiping when we acknowledge His holiness.

So we've answered the first question about worshiping God through prayer, *What does it mean to worship?* It means to acknowledge God's worth, specifically His worth as our Heavenly Father and His worth as our holy God. Let's move on to the next question:

How do I worship God through prayer?

The first way is through giving thanks. When we

thank God, we are acknowledging His worth, because we are expressing our belief that He is the Source of the good things in our life. This is one aspect about worship that helps us keep our vision for life, because it reminds us of all the blessings that surround us.

This is why the Bible says to "give thanks in all circumstances; for this is God's will for you in Christ Jesus" (1 Thess. 5:18). Notice it doesn't say to give thanks *for* all circumstances, but "in all circumstances." In other words, no matter what you are going through, there is always *something* to give thanks for. This is one of the ways we worship God, and one of the ways we keep our vision clear and positive.

Have you ever just spent time thanking God in prayer? If not, I encourage you to. It's a great way to start your prayer time. And it's true worship.

The second way we worship God through prayer is with praise. Praise is closely related to giving thanks, but it is also different. I thank my wife for a birthday gift, but I praise her for what a great job she's done raising our daughters, for how well she plays the piano, and for how pretty she is!

To praise God is to say something good about Him: something good about what He's done ("Lord, that was a beautiful sunset tonight") or to say something good about who He is ("Lord, it's awesome to think of how wise you are"). Jesus once praised God for His mysterious and surprising ways:

At that time Jesus said, "I praise You, Father, Lord of heaven and earth, because You have hidden these things from the wise and learned, and revealed them to little children. Yes, Father, for this was Your good pleasure

(Matt. 11:25-26).

Do you spend time praising God? Just telling Him why you love Him, and how wonderful He is? It's a sure-fire way to brighten your day, and it is worship.

The third way we worship God through prayer is through adoration. Adoration is the part of worship that is reserved for God alone—*worship proper*, if you will. This is that place we come to in worship where we acknowledge God's ultimate worth and understand how far above us He is, and all we can do is bow before Him and, well, *adore* Him. Marvel at Him. Be amazed, humbled, and overjoyed all at once. This is the purest worship, when we're just appreciating God for who He is. This will be our greatest joy in heaven.

We worship God through prayer by giving thanks, by praise, and adoration. Let's look at the third question about worshiping God through prayer:

What will it do for me?

Worship will connect you to heaven. Remember, the key to understanding the Model Prayer is to understand that Jesus would not have told us to pray a prayer that didn't work. Jesus told us to pray in this first verse of the Model Prayer, "Our Father *in heaven*" (Matt. 6:9a, emphasis added). If Jesus told us to address God in heaven, it must mean that we *connect with heaven* when we pray a prayer of worship!

Worship will connect us to heaven. We see this confirmed in other

Scriptures. Psalm 100:4a says, "Enter His gates with thanksgiving and

His courts with praise." The "gates" and "courts" were those of the Old

Testament temple, where God lived in those days. This verse was telling the worshiper how to enter God's presence—with "thanksgiving" and "praise." That is, with worship.

Since the death and resurrection of Jesus, God doesn't live in a physical building anymore. Jesus has made it possible for believers to access His eternal temple in heaven. But the way we do it remains the same: with "thanksgiving" and "praise." With worship. We connect with heaven through worship.

Another Scripture:

*Yet you are **enthroned** as the Holy One; you are the **praise** of Israel* (Ps. 22:3, emphasis added).

Notice the connection between God being "enthroned" (ruling in our lives) and "praise." God comes to sit as Ruler in our lives when we worship Him. The King James Version translates this same verse, *"But thou art holy, O thou that **inhabitest** the praises of Israel"* (emphasis added). God *inhabits*—that is, *lives in*—our praises, our worship. Our worship connects us to Him.

One time an enemy army came to attack Jerusalem (2 Chron. 20). They were too vast an army for the men of Jerusalem to defeat on their own. They went to the temple and prayed, and King Jehoshaphat had an idea. As they went out to face the invaders, he placed singers in front of his army! What were they doing? Singing praises to God. The Bible says they sang, *"Give thanks to the Lord, for his love endures forever"* (2 Chron.

20:21b). So as they marched out to battle, a choir led the way! What happened? Surely they must have been slaughtered.

No, when they reached the battlefield, they found the enemy already dead!

As they began to sing and praise, the LORD set ambushes against the men of Ammon and Moab and Mount Seir who were invading Judah, and they were defeated. The men of Ammon and Moab rose up against the men from Mount Seir to destroy and annihilate them. After they finished slaughtering the men from Seir, they helped to destroy one another. When the men of Judah came to the place that overlooks the desert and looked toward the vast army, they saw only dead bodies lying on the ground; no one had escaped (2 Chron. 20:22-24).

As the people of God worshiped, God Himself came down and fought for them. They won the battle without lifting a sword. Why? Their worship connected them to heaven. God came on the scene and fought their battle for them.

He will do the same for us, for Romans 2:11 says, *"God does not show favoritism."* If you have a battle you need help with, try lifting a song instead of a "sword" (instead of a fist or an angry voice). Your worship will connect you to heaven, and God will come and help you. He is still the One who *inhabits the praises* of His people (Ps. 22:3, KJV).

I discovered the reality of this as a new Christian. As I mentioned earlier, I came to Christ out of atheism. I have never gotten over my amazement at the reality of God, but in the first days and weeks of my new faith I was especially overjoyed. I would go to bed praising and worshiping God out loud, telling Him how much I loved Him, thanking Him, telling Him how beautiful He was. (I lived alone so I could do this out loud without being taken away!)

One night as I lay in bed praising God—for fifteen minutes, thirty minutes?—something strange and wonderful began to happen. What I can best describe as waves of love began pouring over me. I say "waves," though there was no water, because it was weighty and gentle at the same time. It wasn't a *feeling* (though, of course, it caused feelings) because it was something that was *not a part of me* coming over me. It felt wonderful, like I was literally being bathed in love. It was awesome and a little scary. I drifted off to sleep after a while. When I woke up a little while later, it was still happening. I kind of had to ask the Lord to stop—so I could get to sleep.

I believe that was the Holy Spirit being poured out on me. And I believe it was because I was worshiping—my worship was connecting me to heaven. I also believe that every time I worship, or that you worship, the same thing is happening in the spiritual world that happened to me that night. Just because I'm not *feeling* it doesn't mean it's not happening, "for we walk by faith, not by sight" (2 Cor. 5:7, NASB). (I believe God gave me some experiences like that as an atheist-turnedbeliever so I could know the reality of my new faith—and could share it with others).

What will worship do for me? It will connect me to heaven.

SUMMARY

When we lose our vision, we lose our way. One way we keep our vision is through worship. One way we worship, Jesus taught, is through prayer. *What does it mean to worship?* Worship means acknowledging God's worth, specifically His worth as our Heavenly Father and as our holy God. *How do I worship through prayer?* I worship with thanksgiving, praise, and adoration. *What will worship do for me?* It will connect me to heaven—bring God on the scene to bless and help me.

DIGGING DEEPER

Let's dig a little deeper now and see what some other Bible passages have to say about worshiping God through prayer. We'll look at what the Scriptures say, then consider how it applies to our personal lives. There will be a place to record your answers; below that I will give my suggested answers.

If you prefer to continue reading specifically about the Model Prayer, you can turn to Chapter 4 now, and return here later to dig a little deeper.

SAYING THANKS (FROM LUKE 17:11-19)

My wife is a stickler for thank you notes. If we receive a gift, or are invited over to someone's house for dinner, she sends a thank you note. If some church member gives me a gift, she asks me, "Have you sent a thank you card?" I say, "I told him thanks when he gave it to me." She replies, "You still need to send a note."

She also notices when she doesn't receive a note. Perhaps she took a gift to a baby shower, sent a graduation gift to someone, or bought a present for newlyweds. A few weeks go by, and out of nowhere Lynette will say, "You know, I never received a thank you card from _____. I wonder why?" It's not that she's bitter about, but she does notice.

Do you know that God notices whether we say thank you or not? One time when Jesus was on His way to Jerusalem, ten men with leprosy met Him.

They stood at a distance and called out in a loud voice, 'Jesus, Master, have pity on us!" (Luke 17:12b-13).

The reason they stood at a distance is because the Law of Moses required lepers to live away from the rest of society, wear torn clothes, keep their hair unkempt, and cover the lower parts of their faces and cry out "Unclean! Unclean!" if anyone came near them (Lev. 13:45-46).

So these men stood at a distance and called for Jesus to have mercy on them. He did:

When He saw them, He said, "Go, show yourselves to the priests." And as they went, they were cleansed (Luke 17:14).

There were two reasons Jesus told them to go show themselves to the priests. The first reason was to keep the Law of Moses. According to the Old Testament, it was the priests' job to declare "clean" anyone who had been healed of leprosy—to clear them for re-entering society. The second reason was that it required an act of faith on the part of these men. You'll notice in the verse above that they were not healed before they turned to go to the priests, but only "as they went" were they cleansed. They had to obey Jesus' words and take that step of faith before the cleansing came.

All ten were healed. But notice what happened next:

One of them, when he saw he was healed, came back, praising God in a loud voice. He threw himself at Jesus' feet and thanked Him—and he was a Samaritan (Luke 17:15-16).

Though all ten were healed, only one came back and said thank you to Jesus. And the one who came back wasn't even a Jew, one of the chosen people. He was a Samaritan, people who partly worshiped the one true God of the Jews, but who mixed their worship of Him with pagan beliefs. Because of this the Jews ordinarily had nothing to do with them. But it was the Samaritan who came back and gave thanks—the one who might be least expected to.

Jesus noticed:

Jesus asked, "Were not all ten cleansed? Where are the other nine? Was no one found to return and give praise to God except this foreigner?" (Luke 17:17-18).

Jesus noticed that only this one man came back to give thanks. And He wondered why the other nine hadn't. God notices whether we say thank you or not. It's one of the ways that we give Him worship, that we stay connected to Him.

It also keeps our vision for life clear and bright. Have you ever noticed how you can have ninety-nine things going great in your life and one going wrong—and your focus is on the one wrong thing? I know that is often the case with me. I tend to lose sight of all the blessings because of the one or few things going wrong.

The practice of giving thanks will restore our vision. It will help us focus on all the things going well, rather than the one or two things going wrong. "Heavenly Father, it sure is a struggle at work these days. We are overwhelmed, don't have enough help. But thank You that I have a job. Thank You that I have a vehicle to drive to work, a house to go home to. Thank You for my family. Thank You for my health. And a special thank You for my vacation time coming up soon!"

In any situation, we can find much to give thanks for, and it will restore our vision. A man and wife were on a long trip. They stopped at a full-service gas station. After the attendant washed the windshield, the man leaned out of the window and said, "It's still dirty. Wash it again."

The attendant complied. When he finished, the man leaned out the window again, and said, "It's still dirty. Don't you know how to wash a windshield?"

At that, the man's wife reached over, removed her husband's glasses, cleaned them with a tissue, and slipped them back on him—and behold: the windshield was clean!

Sometimes all we need for a brighter day is not the removal of our problems, but the cleansing of our vision. Thankfulness is the cleansing agent.

What is the one problem you've been focusing on?

_____

What are some things you could thank God for instead?

_____

Would other people call you a thankful person?

Remember to include thankfulness in your prayer time and as you go throughout your life. It's one of the ways we worship God, and keep our connection to heaven.

BUILDING THE PRESENCE OF GOD IN YOUR LIFE (FROM PSALM 22:3, KJV)

After God delivered Israel from slavery in Egypt, He took them to the Promised Land, "a land flowing with milk and honey." However, the Promised Land was no picnic; it was filled with enemies. Israel had to defeat these enemies before they could enjoy the milk and honey.

Old Testament Israel is a prophetic type, or symbol, of the New Testament church—the church as a whole, and every believer in it. Their natural experiences parallel our spiritual experiences. Their experiences were recorded in Scripture to teach us, as the Apostle Paul makes clear in the following verses:

For everything that was written in the past was written to teach us, so that through endurance and the encouragement of the Scriptures we might have hope (Rom. 15:4).

These things happened to them as examples and were written down as warnings for us, on whom the fulfillment of the ages has come (1 Cor. 10:11).

Like Israel, we as Christians have been delivered from slavery— from the *spiritual* slavery of sin and guilt. Like Israel, we as Christians have been led to our Promised Land—not a geographical location, but a life of blessed Christian living wherever we call home. (Some have mistakenly assumed the Old Testament's Promised Land to be a symbol of heaven, but there are no enemies in heaven. The Old Testament's Promised Land is a symbol of the blessed Christian life God wants for every believer.) And like Israel, we face enemies seeking to deny us our Promised Land experience—enemies such as temptations, bad habits, discouragements, unkind people, difficult circumstances, financial needs, and the like.

These enemies are meant to frustrate God's good plan for our life. They often arrive just as we're about to make progress of some kind, like when we've taken a step to grow spiritually, when we've just become a Christian, or when we've stepped out in faith to serve the Lord in some way. Things will pop up to make our progress in life, especially our spiritual progress, a challenge. Enemies reside in our Promised Land, just as in Israel's.

How did God prepare Israel for the enemies they would face? On the way out of Egypt, and before they reached the Promised Land, God told Israel to stop in the desert and build Him a home among them. This home was an elaborate tent, called the tabernacle, which allowed God to travel with the Israelites wherever they went. It was the prototype for the later permanent temple built in Jerusalem. It was built according to exact instructions given by God (Ex. 25:9, Heb. 8:5). It was

God's home among the Israelites, and their key to victory in the Promised Land. God Himself was with them, fighting their battles for them, and keeping His word to them (Josh. 23:14).

We also must prepare for our battles by building God a home among us. But we don't do it with an elaborate tent or a lavish temple. We do it with praise. Remember the Scripture we looked at earlier in the chapter:

*But thou art holy, O thou that **inhabitest the praises** of Israel* (Ps. 22:3, KJV, emphasis added).

We build God's presence in our life by praising Him. He *inhabits* that praise. He already lives in us as Christians (see 1 Cor. 3:16 and 1 John 4:15), but His *manifest* presence—His active, life-changing presence— is increased in our life when we praise Him. That manifest presence will defeat our enemies, just like it did Israel's.

Are you facing an enemy? Then I encourage you, both during your prayer time and as you go about your day, to spend time praising God. Say good things about Him. Describe something wonderful He's done, or something wonderful about who He is. Build His presence in your life, and He'll go before you in battle.

A side benefit of a life of praise is the positive attitude it develops in you. You'll be quicker to laugh and show affection. And studies have shown that such positive living can be good for your health.

For example, researchers at the University of Maryland found that laughing patients were healthier patients; specifically, they were less likely to have heart problems. They interviewed 300 patients, asking them questions to measure how they responded to typical day-to-day situations. The patients who tended to respond with laughter were better off. The patients with heart problems were forty percent *less likely* to respond with laughter.

The researchers found that laughter releases chemicals into the bloodstream that relax the blood vessels, and that hearty laughter reduces blood pressure and heart rate. It seems the old axiom "Laughter is the best medicine" is true after all. The Bible agrees: "A cheerful heart is good medicine, but a crushed spirit dries up the bones" (Prov. 17:22).

Another study found that a little marital affection each morning might be the best thing you can do for your health. This study was done by a group of German psychologists, doctors, and insurance companies. Their purpose was to find the secret of long life. The secret? Kiss your spouse each morning before you leave for work! German men who kissed their wives each morning had fewer car accidents on their way to work, missed less work due to sickness, earned twenty to thirty percent more money, and lived five years longer than the non-kissers.

How can a little kiss have such a big impact? Dr. Arthur Szabo put it this way: "A husband who kisses his wife every morning begins the day with a positive attitude."

Don't underestimate the importance of a positive attitude. And it's one of the side benefits of a life of praise. Praise is good for us all around, spiritually, and physically.

Need some help getting started? Try this. In the lines below, write a love letter to God. After all, He wrote one to you (the Bible). I've provided a few phrases to stir your creative juices.

"Dear God,
"I love You because

_____

_____

"You're the only One who can

_____

_____

"I need You in my life because

_____

_____

Love, _____

ABOVE US (FROM GENESIS 1, EXODUS 3, PSALM 139, AND ISAIAH 40)

The Bible says we were created in God's image: "So God created man in His own image, in the image of God He created him; male and female He created them" (Genesis 1:27). To be created in God's image means that He created us to be like Him in a lot of ways, to share a common nature. For example, we can think and reason. We can feel emotions. Most importantly, we can make moral choices. The reason God created us in His image, with things in common, was so that we could know and have fellowship with Him.

The Bible says we were created in God's image, but it does say—it's important to point out—that we were *created.* God is the One who made us, not the other way around. We are dependent on Him for our existence; He is not dependent on us. This reveals an important truth: there are some things we do *not* have in common with God. There are some ways that His nature is above ours, and always will be. It is because of this higher nature of God that we worship Him.

We know God because we were made in His image. We worship God because we were *made*—He is above us.

It is in our response to God's higher nature that adoration, the third way to worship God through prayer, comes in. We simply bow before Him and allow ourselves to be awed, amazed, and overjoyed by Him. This is the purest form of worship—*worship-proper*—and will be our greatest joy in heaven.

There are several ways that God has a higher nature than us. We have already mentioned one that sets Him above us forever: *He is the Creator.* The gulf that separates our nature from the Creator's is illustrated by the story of two scientists who, after discovering how to clone humans, challenged God: "We don't need you anymore. We can make life ourselves now."

God said, "Ok, let's have a man-making contest."

The scientists said, "All right. We'll do it like you did in the beginning."

They reached down to grab a handful of dirt to form it into a man—until they heard God's voice from heaven: "Hold it. Get your own dirt."

People can be "creative" only with what they've already been given— materials, talents, opportunities. Only God can create something out of nothing. The fact that God is the Creator forever puts Him above us and

makes Him worthy of worship.

Another way that God's nature is higher than ours is revealed in His very name. When God appeared to Moses in the burning bush, and told him to go to Egypt to deliver his people, Moses asked Him, "What is your name?" People still believed in many gods in those days, and Moses wanted to know what name to give when the people asked, "Who sent you?" Listen to God's answer:

God said to Moses, "I AM WHO I AM. This is what you are to say to the Israelites: 'I AM has sent me to you'" (Ex. 3:14).

God told Moses, "My name is I Am." In other words, God's basic name is "I Exist." When you think about it, could there be a more profound or important name for the one true God? Isn't His existence the central truth of the universe? And that's His name: "I Am." ("I Am" is "Yahweh" in the Hebrew, or some have rendered it "Jehovah.")

Notice "I *Am*" is His name, not "I came to be." There was never a time God did not exist. No one made Him. *He is eternal.* That is the aspect of His higher nature that His name reveals. And it is truly awe-inspiring. You and I, as *creatures* ourselves, cannot conceive of anyone or anything having always existed. Everything had a beginning. Everything came from somewhere, but not God, according to His name (and many other Scriptures). God always existed. It is humanly inconceivable, and reveals that He is truly in a class all by Himself.

Read the following text and write down what aspect of God's higher nature you see in it:

O LORD, you have searched me and you know me.

You know when I sit and when I rise; you perceive my thoughts from afar.

You discern my going out and my lying down; you are familiar with all my ways.

Before a word is on my tongue you know it completely, O LORD (Ps. 139:1-4).

One aspect of God's higher nature revealed in the above text: _____

(The writer says that God knows everything about Him: when He sits and rises (2), the thoughts in His mind (2), what He's up to (3), and even what He says before He says it (4). This text is referring to God's omniscience, the fact that He knows everything.)

God's omniscience certainly sets Him above us all— especially when it comes to the future. Several years ago, as the turn of the twenty-first century was approaching, I did some research on the predictions that had been made over the years about the year 2000 (for my book *The 100 Most Entertaining Predictions About the 21ˢᵗ Century*). And I found out that when it came to predicting what the future would hold, the best people could do was make some guesses—and some pretty wild ones at that.

One utopian novel, *Looking Backward, 2000-1887* by Edward Bellamy, imagines a man from the 1880s falling into a hypnotic sleep and waking up in the year 2000 to find:

- There is no more housework.
- When it rains, no one gets wet. Instead a huge umbrella is rolled out over the city. It's

considered "an extraordinary imbecility" to let weather affect activity.

- There are no bad marriages, because women refuse to marry unproductive men.
- And sports are for amateurs only—no money, just glory.

Mr. Bellamy was obviously imagining the future through some rose-colored glasses. He wasn't alone. The science editor of the New York Times, in a 1950 *Popular Mechanics* article, also had some rosy predictions for the year 2000: the state-of-the-art home would cost $5,000, every family would have their own helicopter, parked on the roof, and science would have done away with aging (no one looking a day over forty).

The future is a mystery to the human being, but it—and all other knowledge—is an open book to God: "I make known the end from the beginning, from ancient times, what is still to come" (Isa. 46:10a). His omniscience puts Him above us and makes Him worthy of worship.

Read these additional verses from Psalm 139 and write down what aspect of God's higher nature they reveal:

Where can I go from your Spirit? Where can I flee from your presence?

If I go up to the heavens, you are there; if I make my bed in the depths, you are there.

If I rise on the wings of the dawn, if I settle on the far side of the sea,

even there your hand will guide me, your right hand will hold me fast (Ps. 139:7-10).

One aspect of God's higher nature revealed in the above text: _____

(The writer asks where He can go to flee from God's presence (7), and realizes the answer is nowhere—not the highest heights or the lowest depths (8), not the east or the west (9). He is referring to God's omnipresence, the fact that He is everywhere.)

God's omnipresence sets Him above us. He is everywhere, all the time. This is true only of God.

This should also be a great encouragement to us. We're not alone as we make our way through life. God is our companion.

Have you noticed God's presence with you? If not, it's simply because you're not looking for it. Do a little experiment right now. Look around you and find three things with blue in them—articles of clothing, a purse, a book, etc. Take a moment and do that before you read the next paragraph.

What happened after a few seconds of looking for items with the color blue? Everything around you with the color blue in it began to jump out at you, didn't it? Those blue items were there all the time, but you hadn't noticed them because you weren't looking for them.

It works the same with the presence of God. It is with you at all times, but you might be missing it just because you're not looking for it. Start looking for His presence in your life—in your blessings, in your day-to-day pleasures, in your family and friends and church, and even in your struggles (in the strength you're given to make it through them)—and you'll see Him everywhere you go.

Let's look at one more aspect of God's higher nature.

Read the following verses from Isaiah 40, and write down what aspect of God's higher nature they reveal (an aspect, that is, that we haven't discussed yet):

Who has measured the waters in the hollow of his hand, or with the breadth of his hand marked off the heavens? Who has held the dust of the earth in a basket, or weighed the mountains on the scales and the hills in a balance? (Isa. 40:12).

Lift your eyes and look to the heavens: Who created all these? He who brings out the starry host one by one, and calls them each by name. Because of His great power and mighty strength, not one of them is missing (Isa. 40:26).

One aspect of God's higher nature revealed in the above texts: _____

(Verse 12 refers to all of the earth and its great mountains being but dust on God's scales—they weigh nothing to Him. Verse 26 refers to God's control of the mighty stars by His mightier strength. These verses reveal God's omnipotence, the fact that He is all-powerful.)

God's creation and control of the stars is a particularly outstanding display of His power. First of all, there are so many of them. You can see about 3000 stars in the night sky, but in our Milky Way Galaxy there are more than 100 billion stars. That's just our galaxy. There are more than 100 billion galaxies, and each of them has another 100 billion stars or so. That means there are some 10 billion trillion stars in the known universe.

There are about as many stars in the universe as there are grains of sand on all the beaches of the earth.

Second, there's such a great distance between each of these stars. The average distance between the stars in our galaxy is thirty trillion miles. How far is that? Well, the Space Shuttle travels about 17,000 miles per hour, which is about five miles per second. It would take over 200,000 years to travel on the space shuttle from one star to another in our galaxy. Authors Norman L. Geisler and Frank Turek, in their book *I Don't Have Enough Faith to Be an Atheist*, point out that "if you had gotten into the Space Shuttle at the time of Christ and begun traveling from our sun toward another star an average distance away, you would be only one-hundredth of the way there right now." And that's just the distance between two of the stars in our galaxy. Imagine that distance between all of the innumerable stars in the universe—that distance from "one grain of sand on the beach" to another.

And third, each star contains such vast power. Scientists tell us that our sun gets its energy from nuclear fusion reactions that go off in its core, producing temperatures of twenty-seven million degrees Fahrenheit. And our sun is a small star.

These stars—so great in number, so unimaginably distant between, and so powerful—are the handiwork of God. "Because of His great power and mighty strength, not one of them is missing" (Isa. 40:26). He is truly *Almighty* God—far above us and worthy of our greatest adoration.

There are some ways in which we are like God, made in His image. Because of this we can know Him. There are other ways in which God has a nature far above ours. He alone is the Creator; He alone is the eternal "I Am."

He alone is omniscient, omnipresent, and omnipotent.

It is because of His infinitely higher nature that we worship Him.

Chapter 4

CHANGING THINGS THROUGH PRAYER

MY WIFE AND I STARTED dating in our sophomore year of college at a school in Phoenix, Arizona. When spring break rolled around, Lynette went home to visit her family in Yuma, Arizona. While home, she went to get her hair done and fainted in the stylist's chair. They took her to the hospital, and it was discovered that she had internal bleeding.

I was in Phoenix where my family lived and was worried when I heard the news. I wasn't a Christian at the time, however, and I didn't have any kind of belief in prayer. All I could do was hope they figured out what was wrong, and hope she got better.

Lynette's parents, however, were devout Christians. They asked their church to pray for Lynette in their Wednesday night prayer meeting.

They sent word for prayer in other churches, too.

The next day, as the doctor prepared to do exploratory surgery, the mysterious happened—or, as Lynette's parents would say, the miraculous. They ran one last test on Lynette and discovered to their surprise that the internal bleeding had stopped! There was no explanation for it, but the bleeding was gone. Lynette was perfectly fine.

Lynette's parents were convinced that this was an answer to prayer. At the time, I was just pleasantly surprised. Looking back, I realize that God was showing me, even before I was willing to accept it, that *prayer changes things.*

Let's look at the next thing Jesus told us to pray in the Model Prayer:

Your kingdom come, your will be done on earth as it is in heaven (Matt. 6:10).

Many people assume that this is a prayer asking Jesus to return and set up His eternal *"kingdom."* Though there would be no harm in praying for the Lord to return (and every Christian should certainly be looking forward to His return), I don't see how it would do any good— praying for His return, that is. His return is going to happen, and happen at a time already set, whether you or I or anyone prays about it.

Right before His return to heaven after his resurrection, the disciples asked Jesus, *"Lord, are you at this time going to restore the kingdom to Israel?"* (Acts 1:6b). In other words, "Lord, is Your kingdom coming now?"

Jesus answered them, *"It is not for you to know the times or dates the Father has **set** by His own authority"* (Acts 1:7b, emphasis added). Jesus told them that they didn't need to worry about when His kingdom would come; the Father had already "set" that date and He would take care of it.

So the Lord's return is going to happen, and happen at its appointed time. It's not something we need to pray about. We should be looking forward to it, and serving the Lord in light of it, but it's not something we need to pray about.

What did Jesus mean, then, when He told us to pray *"your kingdom come"* if He wasn't telling us to pray for

Him to return and set up His eternal kingdom? He was telling us to pray for the power of His kingdom to come right now in the present age and change things!

This is a very exciting verse if you keep in mind that Jesus would not have told us to pray a prayer that didn't work, and if you understand that He is telling us to pray for the *power* of His kingdom to come right now. It means that every time we ask for his kingdom to come, it must come in some form or fashion! Isn't that amazing?

Prayer changes things!

Why does prayer change things? What kind of prayer do you have to pray to change things? In what ways does prayer change things? Let's address these questions.

Why does prayer change things?

Have you ever wondered why prayer is necessary? If God is allpowerful, all-wise, and all-loving, why doesn't He just do what He wants to do without us praying about it? Why does He expect us to pray? The answer is, God is keeping His word.

In the beginning, when God created human beings, He said to them, *"Be fruitful and increase in number; fill the earth and **subdue** it. **Rule over** the fish of the sea and the birds of the air and over every living creature that moves on the ground"* (Gen. 1:28b, emphasis added). He told the man to *"subdue"* and *"rule over"* the earth. In other words, He gave man *authority* over the earth. God has never taken that authority back; He has never gone back on His word.

God took this word so seriously that He even allowed

Adam to hand over his authority to the devil when Adam chose to—which is what he was doing when he rebelled against God and ate of the forbidden tree (Gen. 2:17, Gen. 3:1-7). The reason for all the evil and suffering in the world is because mankind, through our sin, gave the devil the authority—the legal right, if you will—to work here.

God took His word so seriously that even when it came time to visit the earth through the Virgin Mary and redeem mankind, He first got Mary's consent. The angel Gabriel appeared to Mary and told her of God's plan to bring His Son into the world through her. Mary asked how this could be since she was a virgin. Gabriel said it would happen miraculously, by the power of the Holy Spirit. Mary replied, *"I am the Lord's servant. . . . May it be to me as you have said"* (Luke 1:38a). What I want you to notice is that God did not involve Mary against her will. He waited until she said, "May it be to me as you have said." God refused to enter the world that He had given to human beings until he received a human being's permission!

That's how seriously God takes the delegated authority He has given mankind.

That is why prayer is necessary. It gives God the "legal" right to come and work here. A man or woman, a member of the species to whom God has given the earth, is inviting God in through prayer. Now He is free to come and help us.

The highest heavens belong to the LORD, but the earth he has given to man (Ps. 115:16).

God *could* come and do anything He wants without

us praying for it. But He *won't*. He has given the earth to man (as the above verse states), and He's never taken His word back. He waits to be invited before He works here. We invite Him through prayer.

So why does prayer change things? It gives God the invitation He needs to work on earth on our behalf. The devil is a criminal, and will lie or pressure his way in "to steal and kill and destroy" (John 10:10a). God is a gentleman, and always waits to be invited: *"Here I am! I stand at the door and **knock**. If anyone hears my voice and opens the door, I will come in"* (Rev. 3:20, emphasis added). He is *knocking*. We open the door and invite Him in through prayer.

What kind of prayer do you have to pray to change things?

A prayer that is according to His will. Jesus told us to pray, *"your kingdom come, your **will** be done"* (Matt. 6:10, emphasis added). It is prayer according to God's will that changes things.

So it is important when we pray to find God's heart on a matter. What is it His will to do? What does He want us to pray? This may mean that we should listen first, to discern what God is saying. When we let the Holy Spirit lead our prayers, we'll see things changing.

God can't be manipulated into doing things against His will. There's the story of a boy who wanted a new bike. He decided to pray about it. He paced in his living room, thinking what to pray, and said, "God, if you get me the new bike, I'll be good the rest of my life." He thought, *God will never believe that*. He tried again, "God, if You get me that new bike, I'll be good for three weeks." He thought, *God won't believe that either.* He spotted a statue of the Virgin Mary on the mantle and got an idea. He took the statue to his room, tucked it in a drawer, and returned to the living room. Then he prayed, "God, if You ever want to see your mother again . . . "

We may laugh at that story, but it's pretty common for people to try to manipulate God into answering prayer. Perhaps by how many words we use in our prayer, by how much faith we claim to have, by the Scriptures we quote, and so on. There may be some validity to some of these "prayer formulas," but the bottom line—if we want results in our prayer—is to find God's heart on a matter and pray according to His will.

This is the confidence we have in approaching God: that if we ask anything according to his will, he hears us. And if we know that he hears us—whatever we ask—we know that we have what we asked of him (1 John 5:14-15).

A prayer that changes things must be according to His will.

In what ways does prayer change things?

As we've learned, every time we pray for God's kingdom to come, it *does* come in some form or fashion—in some way His power comes and changes things. But His kingdom does not always come in the same way. It has a few different ways of coming:

Sometimes His kingdom comes with obvious power. At the first church where I served as full-time pastor, the church prayed for a man who was deathly ill in a local hospital, a man named Don. The church didn't know Don personally at the time (he was a friend of one of the members), but the church prayed for him during the Wednesday night prayer meeting. Don later told us what happened in his hospital room.

He was in the bed, near death, when a cloud began to come in the room's window. In the Bible, God sometimes appeared in a cloud (Ex. 13:21; 1 Kings 8:10; Matt. 17:5). But Don wasn't a believer at the time and had no idea what was happening—until a voice spoke to him from the cloud about his need to turn his life over to God, promising to heal him. Then the cloud left.

Don did give his life to God, and he did recover. He later became a member of our church. He said that the miraculous occurrences in his hospital room that night were all because our church prayed for him. The power of God's kingdom had come in the room that night and *changed things* for Don.

Sometimes His kingdom comes with obvious power when we pray.

Sometimes His kingdom comes behind-the-scenes. That is, it may not be obvious for a while that the kingdom came and changed anything when we prayed. We may have to go down the road some before we see any results. But our prayer *did* work—Jesus said it would. It's just not obvious this time. It's behind-the-scenes.

My neighbor, David, told me about an interesting day he had early in his Christian life. He woke up one morning excited about a worship concert he was going to attend that night, praying, "Lord, use me today," and visualizing God using him in worship as he raised his voice with the crowd of people. Things didn't turn out like David expected.

First, he was late for the concert. He took the wrong route and realized he needed to get gas, so he had to pull into a service station. At the station, he looked over and saw a guy about to break his car window with a rock—the man had locked himself out of his car. David said, "Don't break your window. I can help you get in your car." David opened his trunk, pulled out a slim jim, and opened the man's car for him ("Some of my pre-Christian skills came into use there," David told me).

Now, frustrated and angry—and more late than ever—David drove to the concert. But there was no place to park, so he pulled over into a dirt field, which was muddy from rain. When he stepped out of the car, he stepped on a Bible lying there in the mud. He picked it up, and inside it he saw $240 in cash! There was a lady's name in it, so he took the Bible and the cash to the information desk in the lobby, and they said they would get them to the lady.

He was finally at the concert, but now there were no seats left.

He had to stand in the back for the concert. No one greeted him. He stood there upset, wondering what had happened to this day that had started off so well.

It didn't dawn on him until the next day that what had happened to him was his prayer! He had asked God to use him, expecting a great worship experience. God had used him all right, but in a different way: to keep one man from breaking his car window and to return a Bible and $240 to a woman! God's kingdom had come when David prayed, but not in the obvious way. God had worked behind-the-scenes to use him. Sometimes His kingdom comes with obvious power. Sometimes His kingdom comes behind-the-scenes. But—

Always His kingdom comes with His presence. We may not see His kingdom come with obvious power to change things when we pray. We may have to wait a long time to see how our prayer worked behindthe-scenes— maybe even until we get to heaven. But we can always enjoy the presence of His kingdom when we pray. The Bible says:

For the kingdom of God is not a matter of eating and drinking, but of righteousness, peace and joy in the Holy Spirit (Rom. 14:17).

No matter what we see or don't see when we pray, we can always enjoy the presence of His kingdom—His peace and joy.

In fact, this is one of the secret ways God changes things—by changing us. Things may be unraveling around us, but He gives us His peace and joy, and we are able to make it through. We are able to keep our heads and make the right decisions. And we find everything working out in the end.

The 1998 movie *Ruby Bridges* tells the story of the six-year-old girl who, in 1960, became the first black person to attend an all-white school in Louisiana. The movie shows Ruby, escorted by four federal agents, walking through an angry crowd outside the school in New Orleans. As they go up the steps, Ruby suddenly turns around, walks back down the steps, and appears to say something to the crowd. The agents motion for her to come back up the steps, but she stays a moment, her lips still moving. Then she turns and goes in the school.

A psychiatrist who has offered to help the family is

looking on. In the next scene, the psychiatrist and Ruby are sitting alone at her kitchen table, where she is coloring.

He says, "But honey, I saw you talking to them. Did you finally get angry with them? Did you tell them to just leave you alone?" "I didn't talk to them," she said.

"I saw your lips moving," he said.

"I wasn't talking to them," she said. "I was praying for them."

"Praying for them?"

"Yes, I pray for them every day in the car. But I forgot that day."

"Oh. What prayer did you say?"

She put her crayons down, folded her hands, and said, "Please God, forgive these people, because even if they say these mean things. They don't know what they're doing, so You can forgive them, just like You did those folks a long time ago when they said terrible things about You."

One of the ways God changes things is by changing us. His presence comes and gives us the peace and love we need to make it through difficult situations.

Always His kingdom comes with His presence.

Prayer changes things by bringing the power of God's kingdom on the scene—sometimes obviously, sometimes in a behind-the-scenes way, always with His presence.

SUMMARY

Jesus would not have told us to pray a prayer that didn't work. Therefore, when we pray, "your kingdom come," it must always come in some form or fashion!

The power of His kingdom comes and changes things. Why does prayer change things? Because it gives God the invitation He needs to come to earth and work on our behalf. What kind of a prayer changes things? A prayer that is according to God's will. In what ways does prayer change things? Sometimes obviously, sometimes behind-the-scenes, but always with His presence.

DIGGING DEEPER

Let's dig a little deeper now and see what some other Bible passages have to say about changing things through prayer. We'll look at what the Scriptures say, then consider how it applies to our personal lives. There will be a place to record your answers; below that I will give my suggested answers.

If you prefer to continue reading specifically about the Model Prayer, you can turn to Chapter 5 now, and return here later to dig a little deeper.

SIMPLE PRAYER (FROM 1 KINGS 18:16-40)

Albert Einstein said, "When the solution is simple, God is answering."

We have seen in this chapter that prayer is really very simple. What it is at heart—what makes it work—is an invitation to God to come to the earth (the realm He has given to us) and work on our behalf. It's really very simple once you see it.

However, people have a way of complicating prayer. This is evident in one of the most exciting stories in the Old Testament: the confrontation between the prophets of Baal and the prophet Elijah. Baal was an idol from the neighboring nations that the people of Israel were enticed into worshiping. He was purported to be the god who brought rain, good harvests, and fertility—which made him attractive to an agricultural people. Because of his association with the reproductive forces of nature, much immorality was involved in his worship.

And he was popular—especially in the days of Elijah (about 875 B.C.), the prophet of the Lord who confronted the worshipers of Baal. Baal worship had become so fashionable that Elijah declared, "I am the only one of the LORD's prophets left, but Baal has four hundred and fifty prophets" (1 Kings 18:22b).

Elijah wanted the people to return to the one true God, so he called for a contest on Mount Carmel. He had King Ahab summon the people of Israel and the prophets of Baal to the mountain, and he declared to them, "How long will you waver between two opinions? If the LORD is God, follow him; but if Baal is God, follow him" (1 Kings 18:21b). Here is the contest he had in mind: The prophets of Baal were to get a bull, sacrifice it, and put it on some wood. He would do the same with another bull. "Then," he said, "you call on the name of your god, and I will call on the name of the LORD. The god who answers by fire—he is God" (1 Kings 18:24a).

It was a bold challenge, to say the least. The prophets of Baal may have wanted to hem and haw and find a way out. But the people said to Elijah, "What you say is good," (1 Kings 18:24b), and the prophets of Baal had no choice but to accept the challenge.

So the prophets took to praying to Baal. In their efforts to get their prayers answered, they demonstrated a number of faulty prayer practices people still engage in today, *practices that needlessly complicate prayer.*

First, the prophets of Baal complicated prayer by praying to a false image of God:

So they took the bull given them and prepared it. Then they called on the name of Baal from morning till noon. "O Baal, answer us!" they shouted. But there was no response; no one answered. And they danced around the altar they had made (1 Kings 18:26).

The most basic way to needlessly complicate prayer is to pray to a false image of God, a misconception of Him. The prophets of Baal made this mistake. Baal was a figment of their imagination, their idea of what God should be. Archaeologists have found rock carvings of him: a god holding a club in one hand and lightning in the other (because he was the god who brought thunder and storm). This is a false image of God.

They were praying to a god who wasn't there.

People today still have a tendency to worship a false image of God—one of their own making. Like the story of the white guy and the black guy who were arguing over what color God is. The white guy insisted, "God is white!" The black guy said, "No, He's black!" They both died about the same time, stood outside heaven's gate, and were still carrying on their argument.

"I'm glad you're here," the white guy said. "Now you'll see I'm right.

God is white!"

"Now you'll see *I'm* right," the black guy said. "God is black!"

They asked the angel to open the gate. When he did, they heard a big voice say to them, *"Buenas noches!"*

People still have a tendency to worship a false image

Answered Prayer | The Jesus Plan

of God. When we pray to a god who suits our prejudices or fears or questionable lifestyles, we are not really praying to God as He is. God will be slow to answer such prayers—if He will at all—because it would reinforce a misconception about Him.

Are you praying to God as He truly is? That is why He gave us the Bible, so we could know the truth about Him. The two characteristics of His nature that we must keep in mind in order to have a healthy prayer life were addressed by Jesus in the opening line of the Model Prayer:

"Our Father in heaven, hallowed be your name" (Matt. 6:9b).

First, we must keep in mind that He is our *"Father,"* who loves and cares for us, and who wants to hear and answer our prayers. Second, we must keep in mind that He is our *"hallowed,"* or holy, Father, who leads us along an upright path in life. If we will keep both these truths in mind, we will have an accurate image of Him when we approach Him in prayer.

Which of these two basic characteristics of God's nature do you need to be more aware of?

_____

What can you do to grow in this awareness?

_____

The second way the prophets of Baal complicated prayer was with religious ceremony. In order to get an answer to their prayer, "they danced around the altar they had made" (1 Kings 18:26). They weren't dancing for fun. It was their religious ritual, aimed at getting their prayer answered.

Religious ritual is still one of the most common ways people complicate prayer. The ritual might be a certain location or posture in which they must pray, the recitation of particular words—perhaps with the aid of candles or incense—the wearing of certain clothes. Such rituals are not necessarily bad, and sometimes they may aid prayer by setting the mood or building faith in the participants. But they are not really necessary. All that is necessary is an invitation to God to come and work in the world He has given to us.

The prophets of Baal also complicated prayer by trying to earn an answer. When their prayers continued unheeded, they resorted to drastic measures:

So they shouted louder and slashed themselves with swords and spears, as was their custom, until their blood flowed (1 Kings 18:28).

They thought they would earn spiritual favor by making themselves suffer.

This misconception is common. People throughout the ages have flogged themselves with whips, locked themselves away in monasteries, starved themselves, walked long dangerous miles to holy sites, abstained from marriage, given away all their worldly goods, and even blown themselves to bits—all in the hope of winning God's favor.

And all of it unnecessary. Jesus said,

"If you, then, though you are evil, know how to give good gifts to your children, how much more will your

Father in heaven give good gifts to those who ask him!"
(Matt. 7:11).

The only necessity is to understand that God is our
loving heavenly Father who simply desires an invitation
to come and work in our life.

Finally, the prophets of Baal complicated prayer by
adding more and more words, thinking that the length of
their prayer might bring an answer:

Midday passed, and they continued their frantic
prophesying until the time for the evening sacrifice. But
there was no response, no one answered, no one paid
attention (1 Kings 18:29).

They had already prayed "from morning till noon" (1
Kings 18:26). Now they continued praying past midday
"until the time for the evening sacrifice," which was
about 3:00 in the afternoon. Three more hours of begging
for an answer. Talk about a long church service! "But
there was no response, no one answered, no one paid
attention."

A multitude of words isn't necessary for answered
prayer. Remember Jesus' words in His introduction to
the Model Prayer: "And when you pray, do not keep on
babbling like pagans, for they think they will be heard
because of their many words. Do not be like them, for
your Father knows what you need before you ask him"
(Matt. 6:7-8). Jesus said "many words" aren't necessary
to get an answer to prayer. God already knows what we
need. He just needs an invitation to come and work.

The four ways the prophets of Baal complicated
prayer are still ways people complicate prayer today:

praying to a false image of God, thinking religious ceremony must accompany prayer, trying to earn an answer to prayer by suffering or good works, and by adding unnecessary length to prayer. Which, if any, of these complications do you need to watch out for?

The prophets of Baal were unsuccessful in their complicated prayer attempts. No fire came from heaven to consume their sacrificed bull. Now it was Elijah's turn—and he upped the ante! He didn't just go ahead and ask God to send fire to burn up his sacrificed bull, which would seem like a tall enough order. Instead—so the crowd would have no question about the authenticity of what they were about to see—he added stones to the wooden altar his bull lay on, dug a trench around it, and said, *"Fill four large jars with water and pour it on the offering and on the wood"* (1 Kings 18:33b).

Then he told them to pour the water again, and then again—a third time. *"The water ran down around the altar and even filled the trench"* (1 Kings 18:35). It was drenched. Elijah had added stones and water to his offering. He seemed to be stacking the deck against an answered prayer. But watch what happens:

At the time of sacrifice, the prophet Elijah stepped forward and prayed:

"O LORD, God of Abraham, Isaac and Israel, let it be known today that you are God in Israel and that I am your servant and have done all these things at your command. Answer me, O LORD, answer me, so these people will know that you, O LORD, are God, and that you are turning their hearts back again." Then the fire

73

of the LORD fell and burned up the sacrifice, the wood, the stones and the soil, and also licked up the water in the trench. When all the people saw this, they fell prostrate and cried, "The LORD—He is God! The LORD—He is God!" (1 Kings 18:36-39).

The prophets of Baal called on a god of their imagination, danced around their altar, cut themselves, and prayed for hours. There was no answer. Elijah prayed a simple prayer to the one, true God, and a miracle occurred: fire fell from heaven, consumed the sacrifice and wood—even the stones, dirt, and water!

And the people declared, *"The LORD—He is God!"* (39).

True prayer, at its heart, is very simple. It is an invitation to God to come and work in the world He has given to us. The results can be amazing.

"When the solution is simple, God is answering."

ARE THERE FROGS IN YOUR HOUSE?
(FROM EXODUS 8:1-15)

Some people are slow to accept change. Here are some historical examples:

"The horse is here to stay, but the automobile is only a novelty," said a Michigan banker, advising Henry Ford's lawyer not to invest in the new motorcar company.

"Who the (bleep) wants to hear actors talk?" said H. M. Warner, Warner Brothers Pictures.

"Sensible and responsible women do not want to vote," said Grover Cleveland in 1905.

"Heavier than air flying machines are impossible,"

said Lord Kelvin, president, Royal Society.

"Ruth made a big mistake when he gave up pitching," said fellow baseball player Tris Speaker about Babe Ruth.

"There is no likelihood man can ever tap the power of the atom," said Robert Millikan, Nobel Prize winner in physics, 1923.

"Everything that can be invented has been invented," said Charles H. Duell, U.S. Patent Office director, 1899.

Some people are slow to accept change. This can be true even when the change is for their benefit, and it is within their power to make it happen. This was the case with the Pharaoh who held Israel captive in Egypt.

When God sent Moses to deliver Israel from Pharaoh, He gave Moses the power to inflict Pharaoh—and Pharaoh's country—with ten plagues to convince Pharaoh to let God's people go. The second plague was a plague of frogs. Pharaoh was told that if he didn't let the Israelites go:

The Nile will teem with frogs. They will come up into your palace and your bedroom and onto your bed, into the houses of your officials and on your people, and into your ovens and kneading troughs (Ex. 8:3).

Pharaoh did not let them go. So Aaron, Moses' assistant, *"stretched out his hand over the waters of Egypt, and the frogs came up and covered the land"* (Ex. 8:6). They were everywhere: hopping on beds and tables, into drinking cups and eating bowls, down hallways and across the streets. They were being squashed under foot and wheel.

You couldn't get away from them.

Pharaoh gave in. He "summoned Moses and Aaron and said, *'Pray to the LORD to take the frogs away from me and my people, and I will let your people go to offer sacrifices to the LORD'"* (Ex. 8:8).

Moses agreed and said to Pharaoh, *"I leave to you the honor of setting the time for me to pray for you and your officials and your people that you and your houses may be rid of the frogs, except for those that remain in the Nile"* (Ex. 8:9).

Pharaoh responded: *"Tomorrow"* (Ex. 8:10a).

Tomorrow? There are frogs jumping around his legs, the prophet says he'll pray for them to go away whenever Pharaoh wants him to, and Pharaoh says, "Tomorrow"? What about, "Right now, Moses! Pray to get rid of these things right now, please!" But Pharaoh put it off. He was willing to put up with one more night of frogs when he didn't have to—when a prayer would make the difference.

Pharaoh's behavior may bring a smile, but it's possible you and I are doing the same thing—at least from God's point of view. We have learned in this chapter that He has given us the power to change things through prayer, that when Jesus told us to pray, "Your kingdom come," it is because the power of God's kingdom *will* come and change things when we pray. Prayer will work. But how often do you and I put up with adverse circumstances, with things that are obviously not God's will, without bothering to pray about them? We're a lot like Pharaoh when we do that.

Are there some things in your life that need changing? Some "frogs" in your house? It's time to pray about them. In the spaces below, write out a prayer asking God to change a certain adverse situation in your life, and write down the date of the prayer. Later—a day, a week, a month—come back and review your prayer. Then, in the space provided, write down what God has done to change things. I believe you'll be pleased. (In fact, a prayer journal that records your prayer requests and the answers God gives can be a wonderful faith-builder. Consider starting one for yourself.) Prayer changes things.

My prayer: "_____

_____

_____ "

Date of my prayer: _____

What God did in response to my prayer: _____

_____

_____

Date I recognized God's response: _____

Chapter 5

MEETING YOUR NEEDS THROUGH PRAYER

HAVE YOU EVER WONDERED HOW much it costs to raise a child? There are various estimates out there, but all of the estimates agree that it's going to cost a whole lot. On his radio show in 2004, Paul Harvey cited research that estimates it costs about $160,000 to raise a child. Parenthood.com puts the estimate a little higher than that, calculating that it costs $170,000 to raise a child to age eighteen (for a family with a yearly income of about $50,000).

It's expensive to raise a child. Perhaps this is one reason why, when asked in one survey what they would like if their wildest dreams were to come true, more Americans chose winning the lottery (thirty-eight percent) than world peace (one percent).

Financial needs are just one kind of need we have in life. We also have physical needs, relationship needs, and career needs. We have a need for a happy family. We need good health. We need protection.

We need help with various problems we face from day to day.

Having needs is a part of life in this world—it is a part of what makes us human.

The good news is, God wants to meet our needs. The Bible says:

"My God will meet all your needs according to His glorious riches in Christ Jesus" (Phil. 4:19).

God has various ways of meeting our needs. One way is by giving us the ability to work. Another way is by His sovereign providence; He gives us blessings that we in no way earned, such as good parents or talents or opportunities, and so forth. He also meets our needs by rewarding us for being obedient to Him. For example, He said that when we give to Him, He will give to us in return, and more than we gave Him:

"Give, and it will be given to you. A good measure, pressed down, shaken together and running over, will be poured into your lap. For with the measure you use, it will be measured to you" (Luke 6:38).

These are all ways that God meets our needs.

But there's another way God meets our needs: through prayer.

In verse 11 of the Model Prayer, Jesus told us to pray:

Give us today our daily bread (Matt. 6:11).

Here Jesus is telling us that we can pray and ask God to meet our needs. That's what "*daily bread*" is, right? It's food, and food is definitely a need. Jesus told us to pray and ask God to meet our needs.

And, as we've learned, Jesus would not have told us to pray a prayer that didn't work. So, according to the Model Prayer, we can ask that our needs be met through prayer, and expect that prayer to be answered!

But what kind of a prayer results in a need being met? Have you ever prayed a prayer that didn't result in a need being met? I have. Millions of other people have, too.

It's obvious that not all prayer results in needs being met. So what kind of prayer was Jesus referring to?

Let's look at three characteristics of the kind of prayer that meets needs.

A prayer that meets needs *asks.*

"Give us today our daily bread" is a request. It is asking God to meet a need.

It may seem obvious that a prayer that meets needs asks, but as a veteran of many prayer meetings I can tell you that it is not obvious to a lot of people. The prayer meeting may have been called to pray about a specific need in the church—blessing on a certain ministry, money for a new building—but it is surprising how many people will "pray around" the need without ever asking that it be met; or they may "preach a sermon" to the Lord (and the other listeners) about some topic on their heart; or they may pray about all kinds of other things without ever asking for the need to be met.

But not really asking for what you need is nothing new. When the Book of Genesis (the first book in the Bible) comes to an end, Israel is in Egypt. When the Book of Exodus (the next book in the Bible) opens, they are still there—being mistreated as slaves. They're in Egypt for about four hundred years. Here's what's amazing: there is no record in that four hundred year period of them ever asking God to deliver them from slavery.

There's no record of them asking for what they needed until we read in Exodus 2:23b:

"The Israelites groaned in their slavery and cried out,

and their cry for help because of their slavery went up to God."

What happens next? In the very next chapter (just three verses later) God appears to Moses in the burning bush and says,

*"**I have heard them crying out** because of their slave drivers, and I am concerned about their suffering. **So I have come down to rescue them** from the hand of the Egyptians and to bring them up out of that land into a good and spacious land, a land flowing with milk and honey" (Ex. 3:7b-8a, emphasis added).*

Why is God sending Moses to deliver them? They finally asked!

So it's not so obvious—to a lot of people today, and to people in Bible times—that a prayer that meets needs *asks.* Perhaps that is why God tells us directly in James 4:2b, *"You do not have, because you do not ask God."* (The King James Version is even more succinct: *"Ye have not, because ye ask not."*) For some reason, many people are extremely slow about actually asking God to meet a need. They will wander around hurting and lacking for years without really asking for help.

I think one reason for this is that some people just don't know how good God is, and how willing He is to help them. Perhaps they've never witnessed generosity without strings attached, or perhaps all they've known is working hard for what they get. The idea that God will give them something, just because they asked, is hard for them to grasp.

But God really is that kind of God. I noticed this when

I was studying the creation story recently. It dawned on me that Adam's first day on the job was a day off. The Bible says that God made Adam on the sixth day, and gave him a job to do: tend the Garden of Eden and rule over the earth. But what was the next day? The seventh day. And what was the seventh day? The day of rest, of course. So Adam's first day on the job was a day off!

God basically said to him, "Here's your job. But don't come in tomorrow. Take a day off first."

What kind of a boss starts you off with a paid vacation? But that is the nature of God. The Bible says that He is love (1 John 4:8, 16), and it is His nature to give. He *does* want to meet our needs just because we ask.

But we have to ask. That's one characteristic of the kind of prayer that meets needs. Let's look at the second characteristic.

*A prayer that meets needs asks **specifically**.*

"Give us today our daily bread" is a *specific* prayer. It is specific in two ways:

- It is specific in terms of the object that is needed: "Give us today our daily *bread*." It is a request for food.
- It is specific in time: "Give us *today* our daily bread." It is a request for food today.

A prayer that meets needs asks *specifically*. Just as people often wander around in prayer without really asking anything, they often ask too generally. God wants to know exactly what you want.

We see this in a story from Jesus' ministry. Jesus was traveling on the road, a crowd attending Him, when a

82

blind man called out to him:

"Jesus, Son of David, have mercy on me!" (Luke 18:38).

Now it might seem obvious what this blind man wanted Jesus to do for him with His miraculous powers. But look at Jesus' conversation with the blind man:

Jesus stopped and ordered the man to be brought to him. When he came near, Jesus asked him, "What do you want me to do for you?" "Lord, I want to see," he replied.

Jesus said to him, "Receive your sight; your faith has healed you." Immediately he received his sight and followed Jesus, praising God (Luke 18:40-43a).

When the man was brought to Jesus, He asked the man what he wanted. Certainly Jesus already knew, but He required the man to put it into words—to make a specific request. A prayer that meets needs asks *specifically*. God wants to know exactly what you want.

There's a story of the church deacon who had a parrot that would only say, "Let's kiss." He tried to teach his parrot other words, but all it would say was, "Let's kiss. Let's kiss." It embarrassed him. After all, he was a deacon.

The church's pastor also had a parrot, and the only thing it would ever say was, "Let's pray. Let's pray." The deacon thought, *That's more like it. That's how the parrot of a good Christian should talk.* And the deacon had an idea: *I know what I'll do. I'll lend my parrot to the pastor for a while, and his parrot's good manners will rub off on mine.*

The pastor agreed. So they put the deacon's parrot in the cage with the pastor's parrot. Sure enough, the deacon's parrot said, "Let's kiss!" The pastor's parrot replied, "Thank God, my prayers are answered!" Well, there was a parrot that knew what it wanted!

In all seriousness, God wants to know exactly what you want. He wants you to make a specific request.

There is more power in a specific prayer. "Lord, bless me at work" is a good prayer, but "Lord, help me get a raise at work" is a better prayer. "Lord, please bless our troops" is a good prayer, but "Lord, please send an angel to protect my brother as he goes out on patrol today" is a better prayer.

A specific prayer is more powerful for a couple of reasons:

First, a specific prayer is from the heart. God said through the prophet Jeremiah,

*"You will seek me and find me when you seek me with all your **heart"*** (Jer. 29:13, emphasis added).

God pays attention to what comes to Him from our heart. The "heart" refers to our inner person, who we really are. That's the part of us God is listening to. When a prayer comes from our heart, He knows it and responds.

And it is specific prayers that come from the heart, because they express what we really want and need. There's no beating around the bush in a specific prayer.

At the stem of your brain is something called the reticular activating system. It is basically a filter. Every day you're bombarded with millions of stimuli—from things you hear, see, touch, think, etc. If you had to consciously respond to everything your senses picked up, you'd lose your mind. The reticular activating system filters out the inconsequential stimuli, and forwards to your consciousness only what matters.

When it comes to prayer, it seems that God has His own reticular activating system (after all, the Bible calls Him the *Head* of the church— Eph. 4:15). He filters out the inconsequential prayers—empty ones and merely religious or ritualistic ones. He listens to prayers from the heart.

Man looks at the outward appearance, but the LORD looks at the heart (1 Sam. 16:7b).

A specific prayer is more powerful because it comes from the heart.

Second, a specific prayer is more powerful because it requires faith. The Bible is clear that it is faith that moves the hand of God. Jesus said, *"I tell you the truth, if you have faith as small as a mustard seed, you can say to this mountain, 'Move from here to there' and it will move."* (Matt. 17:20b). And the Bible is clear that it is faith that pleases God: *"And without faith it is impossible to please God"* (Heb. 11:6a).

God is looking for faith. A prayer like "Lord, bless me at work" is too general. It may not be obvious whether that prayer is answered or not. That prayer doesn't require much faith. But a prayer like, "Lord, help me get a raise at work" is specific. It *will* be obvious whether that prayer is answered. That prayer takes faith.

A specific prayer is more powerful because it requires faith, and faith moves "mountains."

Pray specifically. Dallas Theological Seminary is one of the largest and most influential schools in the world. Thousands of its graduates serve as Bible-believing ministers throughout the United States and in about one hundred other countries. But the school almost folded before it got off the ground.

Shortly after its first class of thirteen students arrived in 1924, for all practical purposes the school was bankrupt. Creditors were calling for money that wasn't there, and the lenders notified the school that they would foreclose at noon on a certain day. That day the school's board of directors met in the president's office to pray. They believed it was God's will to launch the Bible-believing seminary, but as the minutes ticked toward noon it looked impossible.

In the prayer meeting was Harry Ironside, who would later serve as pastor at Chicago's Moody Memorial Church. He was known for his down-to-earth preaching and praying. When it was his turn to pray, he said, "Lord, we know that the cattle on a thousand hills is thine. Please sell some of them and send us the money."

About the same time, a tall Texan in boots and an open-collar shirt strolled into the business office of the seminary. "Howdy!" he said to the secretary. "I just sold two carloads of cattle over in Fort Worth. I've been trying to make a business deal go through, but it just won't work. I feel God wants me to give this money to the seminary. I don't know if you need it or not, but here's the check."

The secretary took the check, looked at it twice, then went and knocked on the president's door. She handed the check to President Chafer, who also did a double take—because the check was for the exact amount they owed the creditors. President Chafer turned and said, "Harry, God sold the cattle."

The power of a specific prayer. It comes from the heart. It requires faith.

What do you need? Ask for it specifically.

Let's look now at the third characteristic of the kind of prayer that meets needs.

*A prayer that meets needs asks **according to God's plan for our life**.*

A prayer that meets needs not only *asks*, and asks *specifically,* but it also asks *according to God's plan for our life.* What I mean is, some things we're asking for, which we think are needs, are not needs according to God's plan for our life. If He were to meet those "needs," it would actually throw us off course.

I experienced this when I was fresh out of college with a teaching degree. My plan was to teach high school English. For a year and a half, I looked for a teaching position with no results. I applied at public and Christian high schools. I even applied at a school for troubled kids (where applicants weren't exactly beating down the door). I had positive interviews. I was in demand as a substitute teacher. I was qualified, but no one offered me a contract.

Here's what I want to point out: I was praying the whole time! I was praying with full confidence that a teaching job was a "need" I had. I was praying trustingly, and I was trying to live an obedient Christian life. But no one offered me a contract. It was very frustrating.

I couldn't explain it then, but I think I can now. Something was happening inside me during that year and a half. I was beginning to wonder if I was being called into the ministry. I wasn't against the idea. As a new Christian, I could think of nothing more exciting than spending my time talking to people about Jesus. However, I had a hard time believing God could really want me.

Finally, in prayer one night, the call became clear to me. I said yes to God and went to bed happy.

Guess what happened the next morning? A principal called me about a job! I told her, "Thanks, but I'm going into the ministry." She said, "Oh. That's wonderful."

My point is, what if God had answered my prayer and met my "need" for a teaching contract at some point in that year and a half when I was looking for one and praying for one? I may have never entered the ministry. At the very least, I would have had a much harder time hearing and saying yes to His call. I may have missed out on God's best plan for my life.

A prayer that meets needs asks *according to God's plan for our life.*

Have you been praying for a "need" to be met, and nothing's happening?

Maybe you're asking for a job that He doesn't want you to have, that wouldn't be best for you. Maybe you're asking for a relationship with a certain person, which would actually turn out disastrous. Maybe you're asking to be removed from a difficult set of circumstances, but God wants you to stay where you are and be of service. God may not be answering that prayer because it's not according to His plan for your life. It's something to consider. He loves you, and He knows best.

SUMMARY

We all have needs—it's a part of being human. The good news is, God wants to meet our needs. One way He meets our needs is through prayer. What kind of prayer results in needs being met? A prayer that asks. A prayer that asks specifically. A prayer that asks according to God's plan for our life.

DIGGING DEEPER

Let's dig a little deeper now and see what some other Bible passages have to say about meeting your needs through prayer. We'll look at what the Scriptures say, then consider how it applies to our personal lives. There will be a place to record your answers; below that I will give my suggested answers.

If you prefer to continue reading specifically about the Model Prayer, you can turn to Chapter 6 now, and return here later to dig a little deeper.

DON'T GIVE UP (FROM LUKE 18:1-8)

If we have prayed for a need to be met, and it hasn't been met, should we keep praying about it? What is the answer to that question, according to Luke 18:1?

Then Jesus told His disciples a parable to show them that they should always pray and not give up" (Luke 18:1).

According to this verse, we should persist in prayer if a need hasn't been met.

The parable was about a widow in a certain town who

was not getting justice from some "adversary" (Luke 18:3b). Jesus did not say who the adversary was, or what the conflict. But we can assume that, being a widow, the woman was being taken advantage of by a more powerful or wealthy citizen. She went to the town's judge and said, *"Grant me justice against my adversary"* (Luke 18:3b).

The problem was, the judge was an unjust man. Jesus described him as a man *"who neither feared God nor cared about men"* (Luke 18:2). So when the woman brought her complaint to him, he refused to help her. He just sent her home. Not just once—this went on *"for some time"* (Luke 18:4a).

The woman, however, did not give up. She kept returning, asking for justice. Finally the judge said to himself, *"Even though I don't fear God or care about men, yet because this widow keeps bothering me, I will see that she gets justice, so that she won't eventually wear me out with her coming!"* (Luke 18:4b-5). The judge granted her justice not because she deserved it, but because she persisted in her request. Jesus said there was a lesson about prayer to learn from her story:

"Listen to what the unjust judge says. And will not God bring about justice for his chosen ones, who cry out to him day and night? Will he keep putting them off? I tell you, he will see that they get justice, and quickly. However, when the Son of Man comes, will he find faith on the earth?" (Luke 18:6-8).

The lesson was that persistence in prayer pays off. If an unjust judge will grant justice to a persistent petitioner, how much more so will the just and loving

God of the universe meet the needs of those "who cry out to Him day and night!" When it comes to praying for a need, we should not give up.

As we've discussed before, there are times God will say "No" to a prayer. In those cases, we should not keep praying about the same thing, but should conclude that our request must not have represented a real need after all, that our prayer did not line up with God's will for our life. But when we're praying for a real need, we can assume it is God's will to meet it (Phil. 4:19), and in those cases we should persist in prayer.

There are three ways we can persist in prayer when a need hasn't been met. *One way, of course, is to repeat the request.* It's not that God needs to hear it again. It's that our heart needs to say it again. We are still burdened with it and need to release it to God again, exercising our faith in His help once more.

The second way to persist in prayer is to adjust our prayer. That is, as we seek the Lord for a need to be met, we may sense that we haven't been praying for exactly the right thing to happen. Maybe we've been praying for a raise with no results, when we realize that what we should be praying for is our employer's business to do better. We're still praying for the need to be met, but have been led by the Holy Spirit to pray more specifically. I'll talk more about the need to search our heart in prayer in the following section.

The third way to persist in prayer is with praise and thanksgiving. You know the answer has already been given—you have God's word on it in the Bible, you sense it by the leading of His Spirit. In this case, it doesn't make sense to ask the Lord for it again, or to adjust your prayer. When the need comes to mind, you simply thank Him and praise Him that the answer's coming. This is a form of persisting in prayer.

If we have prayed for a need to be met, and it hasn't been met, we have need of persistence. You may have heard athletes speak of a "second wind," a new burst of energy that comes during a long session of exercise. It's not a myth. According to Dr. Paul G. Donohue, a marathon runner will have depleted all of his muscle glycogen (muscle sugar) at about the two-hour mark. His body will then switch to a new fuel source—fat. Initially, there is fatigue as lactic acid builds up and blood sugar drops. But when the body adapts to the new source of fuel, new energy comes—a "second wind." But the athlete must persist through the fatigue stage to reach the "second wind."

Likewise, there are some prayer rewards that only come to the persistent, to those who refuse to stop trusting that a just and loving God will meet their needs.

Do you have a need that you have prayed about, that hasn't been met yet? Which of the three ways to persist in prayer do you need to practice—repeating the request, adjusting the prayer, or thanking God that the answer is on the way?

SEARCHING YOUR HEART IN PRAYER
(FROM 1 SAMUEL 1:1-2:11)

In the early days of one of the churches I pastored, we met in a movie theater. It was a tough situation for us: there was poor lighting and no place for classes. They moved us to different theaters each week, and one time a movie started in the middle of services. Some theaters weren't airconditioned—which is a problem in Phoenix in the summer.

Then the owners raised the rent on us. We were a small church living out of a trailer, and the increase ate us up. We were not able to deposit any money into our Building Fund, which meant we were not making any progress toward our future.

I decided I needed to ask the owners to lower the rent. First, however, I prayed about it, asking God to give us favor with the owners. After all, we were doing His work, and this was a need we had. Surely He would work on our behalf.

I approached the owners and pled our case, and their answer was very clear: "No."

I was disappointed. To be honest with you, I felt like God had let me down. I know enough to know that God can't ever *really* let me down. He's perfect, and always does what is right and good. But sometimes you can *feel* something when you *know* better.

But that's not the end of the story. The theater owners' "No" caused me to begin to search my heart. I began to wonder if God might be leading us to look for another place to meet. I talked it over with our music minister one afternoon on the phone, and we decided that we should look into meeting at a nearby school that had just built a new cafetorium (as they called it). I hung up the phone, turned on the TV, and there was a news story about that very school! A positive story about a new anti-drug program. A coincidence?

We rented the school and began holding services there, and our church began to take off. People from the community came to Christ. Our attendance doubled. Our finances increased. We went from being a "mission"—a fledgling congregation dependent on a parent church for its survival—to being a real church in our own right, able to stand on our own.

My point is that all of this happened because God had not met the "need" we had prayed about. Because the theater owners said, "No," we began to search our hearts and adjust our prayer to line up with God's real plan for our church: a move to a new location.

If a need you have prayed about has not been met, it could be that you need to adjust your prayer. As we have learned in this chapter, the third characteristic of a prayer that meets needs is a prayer that asks *according to God's plan for our life.* If your prayer has not been answered, search your heart to see if you need to adjust your prayer to line up with God's real plan for your life.

A lady in the Bible did this. Her name was Hannah, and she was one of two wives of a man named Elkanah. Hannah's need was to become pregnant and have a child. Not only did she have the natural desire for a child, but she wanted to escape the social stigma that came from being childless in her society—it was considered a curse from God.

In addition, her husband's other wife, who did have children, "kept provoking her in order to irritate her" (1 Sam. 1:6). You can imagine.

Year after year, when this family *"went up to the house of the Lord"* (1 Sam. 1:7) to worship, Hannah presented her request for a child to the Lord. But the prayer had never been answered, and *"her rival"*—the other wife—*"provoked her till she wept and would not eat"* (1 Samuel 1:7b). Her husband said to her, *"Hannah, why are you weeping? Why don't you eat? Why are you downhearted? Don't I mean more to you than ten sons?"* (1 Sam. 1:8).

Finally the year came when Hannah prayed the prayer that resulted in her giving birth to a son. She stood weeping in front of the house of the Lord and prayed:

O LORD Almighty, if you will only look upon your servant's misery and remember me, and not forget your servant but give her a son, then I will give him to the LORD for all the days of his life (1 Sam. 1:11).

She had prayed year after year for a son, but now she adds a promise. What is the promise?

_____

_____

(She promises that she will give the son back to God.)

What did this mean, that she would give her son back to God? Her husband was a Levite, meaning he belonged to the priestly clan in Israel. Any son he had would also belong to the priestly clan, and be obliged by the Law of Moses to be available for service at the house of God from age twenty-five to fifty. What Hannah was promising was that she would make her son available for service at the house of God from childhood.

This prayer worked:

So in the course of time Hannah conceived and gave birth to a son. She named him Samuel, saying, "Because I asked the LORD for him" (1 Sam. 1:20).

Hannah kept her promise. After raising Samuel for a few years, she took him to the house of the Lord to be apprenticed to the high priest Eli. Samuel would grow into a great prophet, who would shepherd Israel through the transition from a confederation of tribes into a kingdom. He would be in a position to accomplish these things as a result of growing up at the house of the Lord, the center of Israel's religious and political life. And he would be there because Hannah had kept her promise and given him to the Lord.

It had always been God's intention to answer Hannah's prayer for a son. But He had a special plan for that son, a plan that required Hannah to dedicate her boy to the Lord. So He waited until Hannah, after years of disappointment, finally searched her heart and prayed according to God's plan for her life. When she said yes to this plan, the answer came.

Do you have a prayer that hasn't been answered yet? In the space provided, write down what you plan to do with the answer when it comes. Then ask yourself whether your plans will glorify God or not.

It was this issue that was holding up the answer to Hannah's prayer.

Your plans for the answer when it comes:

_____

Will your plans glorify God?

_____

Again, we have learned in this chapter that there are three characteristics of the kind of prayer that results in needs being met: a prayer that *asks*, that asks *specifically*, and that asks a*ccording to God's plan for our life*. Hannah had *asked* (for a child). She had asked *specifically* (for a son). Finally, she searched her heart and asked *according to God's plan for her life*. Then her need was met.

What about you? If a need has not been met, search your heart to see if you are praying according to God's will for your life.

BEYOND PRAYER (FROM JOHN 6:1-14)

The Feeding of the Five Thousand is one of the most famous miracles in the Bible. Jesus was ministering to a large crowd in a remote area where there was no food. He asked His disciples how they were going to feed such a large crowd. The Bible says He only asked this question to test them. He already knew what He was going to do. One disciple said it would take eight months wages to buy enough food for all these people, which may not have been an exaggeration. You see, there were actually more than 5,000 people there. The "5,000" this miracle is known by refers to just the men who were present. The Bible says that there were also women and children there (Matt. 14:21). Where you have 5,000 men, you probably have at least 5,000 women, and maybe another 10,000 kids. So there were likely some 20,000 people there. Eight months' wages may not have fed them.

Another disciple pointed out that there was a boy present who had five loaves of bread and a couple of small fish, but how far could they go? Jesus was about to show him:

Jesus then took the loaves, gave thanks, and distributed to those who were seated as much as they wanted. He did the same with the fish.

When they had all had enough to eat, he said to his disciples, "Gather the pieces that are left over. Let

97

nothing be wasted." So they gathered them and filled twelve baskets with the pieces of the five barley loaves left over by those who had eaten.

After the people saw the miraculous sign that Jesus did, they began to say, "Surely this is the Prophet who is to come into the world" (John 6:11-14).

Jesus took the relatively small gift that was given to Him, miraculously multiplied it, and met the large crowd's need.

The Feeding of the Five Thousand is the only miracle from Jesus' ministry that is recorded in all four Gospels: Matthew, Mark, Luke, and John. Why is that significant? Because when God repeats a matter four times, He's telling us: "This is important." God is teaching this truth through this miracle: If we give to the Lord, He will multiply our gift, and meet the need. Very simple. Very profound.

This reveals that sometimes, when it comes to meeting a need, we need to do more than pray about it. There's an action we need to take first: giving. Jesus took what the boy gave Him, multiplied the gift, and then met the need. Sometimes we need to go beyond prayer to giving to have our needs met.

Sadie Sieker was a house-parent for missionaries' children in the Philippines. Sadie loved books. Some she gladly loaned out, but others she treasured in a footlocker under her bed. One night she heard a faint gnawing sound. After a search, she found the noise was coming from the footlocker. She opened it and found an enormous pile of dust—all the books she'd kept for herself had been lost to termites.

Her story illustrates a Biblical truth: What we try to

hold on to, we often lose. When we give, we receive. As Proverbs 11:24 puts it, *"One man gives freely, yet gains even more; another withholds unduly, but comes to poverty."*

Our church experienced the power of giving. We had searched for land for a church building for years with no success. Either the land was priced too high, the developer wasn't selling to churches, or the land was out of our target area—too far for our people to drive. Land in the growing Phoenix area is always at a premium. We happened to be searching for land at a time when land values were increasing. We found nothing—for five years.

Then we had our "Journey to Joy" fundraising campaign to raise money to buy land (should we find it) and construct a building. We asked the leaders in our church, pastor included, to give to the campaign first—to set an example to the members. We asked everyone to give a one-time cash offering, and then over the next three years to pledge what they could give on a monthly basis.

The most amazing thing happened after we took that offering.

One piece of property after another began to open up for us. Property in our target area, property we could afford, and property in good locations. The major land developer in our area actually invited us into their office to look at their map and pick out the land we wanted.

"A church can go anywhere," the vice president said to us. We ended up purchasing our land from this company, and they sold it to us at a discounted price (because we were a church).

There is a power in giving. Have you been asking God

to meet a need? Perhaps there's an action He wants you to take first. Sometimes we have to go beyond prayer to giving to meet our needs.

Chapter 6

BEING FREE THROUGH PRAYER

SHE CAME TO MY OFFICE for counseling. She was a successful businesswoman—intelligent, attractive, personable—but she wouldn't tell me what she wanted counseling about. She came a number of times, and we talked about various things, but I could tell we were skirting around the real issue.

Then one day I asked her, "Have you had an abortion?" That was it, the real issue. Tears streamed down her face. Her boyfriend—former boyfriend now—had pressured her into it, but she had gone along with it. She was so ashamed that she couldn't even bring herself to mention it.

She looked more hopeless than perhaps anyone I've ever seen. This was startling, since on the outside she had so much going for her. But inside she had no hope. She had taken a life, an innocent life, her own baby's life. How could she live with herself? How could she face God? Guilt had robbed her of hope.

It was my joy to share with her from the Bible how she could have a new start in life, how God would not only forgive her sin but forget it:

*"For I will forgive their wickedness and will **remember their sins no more**"* (Heb. 8:12, emphasis added).

She became a changed person as she accepted this truth. She was eager to read the Bible and learn more about such a loving, forgiving God. She told me I could refer other women in her predicament to her for help (an offer I took her up on)—you know you've been healed when you become a healer! Hope and joy bubbled out of her. She had truly found new life through God's forgiveness.

She had been set free!

There is no prison like the prison of guilt. Psychiatrist Karl Menninger said that if you could convince patients in psychiatric hospitals that their sins were forgiven, seventy-five percent of them would walk out the next day. Forgiveness frees us—from guilt, fear, denial, rationalizations, masquerades, and stress. When we know we are forgiven, we can stop running—from God, from others, from ourselves.

Forgiveness frees us, and here's the amazing thing: we can be free through prayer. In verse 12 of the Model Prayer, Jesus told us to pray:

"Forgive us our debts, as we also have forgiven our debtors" (Matt. 6:12).

Jesus would not have told us to pray a prayer that didn't work. If He said we could ask God to *"forgive us our debts,"* it's because that's what God will do when we ask Him. We can be free of guilt through prayer.

But don't pass over the second thing Jesus told us to pray in this verse: "as we also have forgiven our debtors." Not only can we be forgiven through prayer, we can forgive others through prayer—and free ourselves of the poisonous emotions that imprison us when we refuse to forgive.

In this line of the Model Prayer, Jesus is telling us

how to be free through prayer—free from our own guilt, and free from the emotional baggage caused by other people's sins against us. Let's look at both of these dimensions of freedom.

HOW CAN WE BE FREE OF GUILT THROUGH PRAYER?

By asking! Jesus told us to pray, *"Forgive us our debts."* Because we know that Jesus would not have told us to pray a prayer that didn't work, we know that when we ask God to forgive us, He will.

How can God forgive me just for asking? Don't I have to do something to earn my forgiveness? Don't I have to become a monk, or give a bunch of money away, or fast for a week, or punish myself in some way? How can forgiveness be so free—just for asking?

The reason God is able to freely *"forgive us our debts"* just for asking is because our debts have already been paid for at the cross. When Jesus died on the cross, He declared, *"It is finished"* (John 19:30). In the Greek, the language of the New Testament, *"It is finished"* is *teleo*. An alternate translation for *teleo* is "paid in full." With His death, Jesus was paying in full the debt for our sin. Because Jesus has paid the debt for our sin, God is able to freely forgive us when we ask Him. Forgiveness is free because someone else already paid for it. It cost Him, but it's free to us.

What does this mean to you if you're already a Christian? You don't have to let your failures separate you from your relationship with God. The natural instinct when we sin is to hide in shame from God. This is what Adam and Eve did after the first sin:

*"Then the man and his wife heard the sound of the LORD God as he was walking in the garden in the cool of the day, **and they hid from the LORD God** among the trees of the garden"* (Gen. 3:8, emphasis added).

Sin makes us ashamed and afraid before a holy God. But because Jesus has paid our debt for us, we can run to God when we sin, ask Him to *"forgive us our debts,"* and He will.

What does this mean to you if you're not yet a Christian? You can come to God for forgiveness right now. Jesus has paid your debt! Forgiveness is available to you if you'll just ask:

"For whosoever shall call upon the name of the Lord shall be saved" (Rom. 10:13, KJV).

Does this sound like a wise policy to you, this free forgiveness that God offers? Many object to it, feeling that it gives people a license to sin. But it is the plain teaching of the New Testament, and there are some profound reasons for the free offer of forgiveness:

- The first and foremost reason, as has been previously discussed, is that our debt has already been fully paid by Jesus on the cross. If it's been fully paid, then we owe nothing. Forgiveness is free to us because Jesus paid the price.
- The offer of free forgiveness leaves no room for pride. The devil's fall and man's fall were both due to pride (see Isaiah 14:12-15 and Genesis 3:1-8, respectively). Pride must be left behind to come back into a right relationship with God.

Free forgiveness leaves no room for pride. No one in heaven will be able to say, "I'm here because I did such and such." No, we will be in heaven only because of what Jesus did for us.

- Free forgiveness changes the heart. When we realize that God has freely forgiven us, at a cost to Him alone (the death of His Son), we can't help but be grateful and want to live for Him. It changes the heart.

The night I prayed to accept Christ as my Savior, I hesitated right before I did. My worry was, Will I be able to stick it out? Will I be able to live the Christian life? I don't want to be a hypocrite. But I took the chance and prayed the prayer.

The next day I woke up to a surprise: I wanted to live for God. I wanted to pray, read the Bible, quit the obvious sins, and go to church. I wanted to do these things for the One who had forgiven me so much.

It wasn't going to be a burden at all. My heart had been changed.

You can be free of guilt just by asking. If you're a Christian who has messed up, just ask for forgiveness. Quit running off and hiding behind the bushes! Run to God. If you're not yet a Christian, before you put this book down, bow your head and accept the gift of forgiveness God offers. You can pray this prayer:

"Dear Lord Jesus, I admit that I'm a sinner and need your forgiveness. Thank you for loving me in spite of my sin, and dying on the cross to pay my debt for sin. I ask you to forgive me of all my sins. I ask you to come in my heart and help me to live for you. Thank you for hearing my prayer and saving me for all eternity. Amen."

We can be free of guilt through prayer. That's the first dimension of freedom we can experience by praying this line of the Model Prayer.

HOW CAN WE BE FREE OF EMOTIONAL BAGGAGE THROUGH PRAYER?

We can be free of emotional baggage by forgiving others. After telling us to pray, *"Forgive us our debts,"* Jesus also told us to pray, *"as we also have forgiven our debtors."*

Have you been hurt by someone? I'm sure you have. I don't think it's possible to live on fallen planet earth and get by without being hurt. Some have been hurt more than others, but all people have been hurt.

If you've been hurt by someone, then you know it's a burden. It weighs on your heart. It may have changed your whole life. But there is a way to be free of it: by forgiving the one or ones who hurt you, which you can do through prayer—for Jesus told us to pray, *"as we also have forgiven our debtors."*

It is vitally important for us to forgive others. That is why this is the only part of the Model Prayer that Jesus tagged with a comment. Immediately after the Model Prayer, He said:

"For if you forgive men when they sin against you, your heavenly Father will also forgive you. But if you do not forgive men their sins, your Father will not forgive your sins" (Matt. 6:14-15).

If we don't forgive others, Jesus said, the Father won't

forgive us. That's a sobering thought. Are you holding someone's sins against them? Guess what? God is holding your sins against you. Like I said, a sobering thought.

In what sense does God hold our sins against us if we don't forgive others? Not in an eternal sense. He promised we would be eternally saved if we put our faith in Jesus, and He wouldn't contradict Himself. Our sins will be held against us in an experiential sense; that is, we won't experience all the blessings that are ours because of God's forgiveness of us, blessings such as peace and joy, answered prayer, and intimacy with God. Our unforgiveness toward others disrupts our connection with heaven.

Have you been seeking an answer to prayer and nothing has happened? Check your forgiveness toward others. If you're withholding it, God may be withholding a blessing from you.

It is vitally important that we forgive—for our sakes.

Now I realize it's not always easy to forgive. Perhaps you've heard the story of the woman summoned for jury duty, who said to the judge, "Your Honor, I can't serve on a jury. I don't believe in capital punishment." The judge said, "Ma'am, this isn't a capital charge so that doesn't matter. This is a case where a husband emptied out the wife's savings account of $14,000 to take a 3-day weekend with his girlfriend in Atlantic City." The woman said, "Okay, I'll serve. And I could be wrong about capital punishment."

Or the story of the woman who, after a long illness, died and arrived at the gates of heaven. She looked through the gates and saw the streets of gold and a beautiful banquet table with her friends and relatives rejoicing around it. "What a wonderful place," she said to Saint Peter, who was there to greet her. "How do I get in?"

Peter said, "You have to spell a word."

"What word?" she asked.

"Love," said Peter.

She spelled it and was ushered in.

Sometime later, as the story goes, Peter asked the woman to watch the gates of heaven for a day. It so happened that her husband arrived while she was there. She said, "I'm surprised to see you. How have you been?"

He said, "I've been doing great since you died. I married the beautiful young nurse who took care of you when you were ill. Then I won the lottery. I sold the little house you and I lived in and bought a big mansion. My new young wife and I traveled all around the world. We were on vacation, and I went water skiing today. I fell and hit my head, and now I'm here. How do I get in?"

"You have to spell a word."

"What word?" he asked.

"Czechoslovakia."

As I said, it is not always easy to forgive. **There are three truths to keep in mind to help us forgive:**

First, when we forgive, we're not condoning the act that hurt us; we're forgiving the person who did it.

Many can't forgive because they feel like it will put a stamp of approval on what was done to them. But God is not asking you to approve of the act. He is asking you to forgive the person who did it.

You may have been abused as a child. When you hear the command to forgive, that memory comes to mind, and you think, How can I forgive that? It was evil. You're right, and God is not asking you to condone the act, or to not think of it as evil. He is not asking you to pretend the memory doesn't hurt you, or to pretend that there weren't negative consequences in your life because of it. He's asking you to forgive the person who did it.

Second, when we forgive, it doesn't mean the other person is "getting away with it."

Many can't forgive because it offends their sense of justice. But we don't need to worry about this. There's a spiritual law that rules in the affairs of earth, the law of sowing and reaping:

Do not be deceived: God cannot be mocked. A man reaps what he sows (Gal. 6:7).

According to the law of sowing and reaping, every act is like a seed sown in the ground. That seed will bring forth a harvest for the sower—maybe soon, maybe down the road. But a harvest will come. No one gets away with anything. We can forgive, leaving judgment up to God. *"It is mine to avenge; I will repay," says the Lord* (Rom. 12:19).

Third, when we forgive, we are freeing ourselves.

The ironic thing about refusing to forgive is that we're allowing the original wrong done to us to continue to hurt us through our resentment and bitterness. We're allowing it to keep us in an emotional and spiritual prison. It is through forgiving that we free ourselves.

One of the happiest people in my church, an energetic senior citizen named Betty, had no right to be. Or so it would seem. After eighteen years of marriage and a few children, her husband ran off with another woman—and the other woman was her sister.

They ran off permanently, leaving Betty and the children behind. Betty was devastated, betrayed by the two people closest to her. She was, understandably, bitter to the bone. She said, "When I die, I'm going to be cremated, and send the ashes to my sister with best wishes!"

Some time later, she visited her son in Washington, and went to a church service with him. The preacher's topic: forgiveness. Betty talked to him afterward, telling him what her sister had done. Certainly the preacher couldn't mean her? But the preacher asked her if her sister was still alive. Betty said she was, and the preacher said, "Well, Betty, I think you should tell her that you forgive her. It's not hurting her. It's hurting you."

And Betty did! She went to Oklahoma and told her sister that she forgave her. She forgave her ex-husband as well.

Betty would tell you that, next to receiving Jesus as her Savior, this act of forgiveness is the most important thing she ever did. She said she felt wonderful after doing it, like a weight had lifted from her shoulders. It set her free. She would not have been the happy person she was if she had not forgiven.

When we forgive, we are freeing ourselves.

Is there someone you need to forgive? You can do it right now through a prayer.

SUMMARY

There is no prison like the prison of guilt. We can be free of guilt through a prayer for forgiveness. Forgiveness is ours for the asking because Jesus has paid the debt for us. We can also forgive others through prayer—and free ourselves of the emotional baggage caused by their sins against us. It's not easy to forgive, but we must if we want to experience all the blessings God has for us. It will help us to forgive if we keep in mind that we're forgiving the person, not condoning the act; no one really "gets away" with anything. And when we forgive, we're freeing ourselves.

DIGGING DEEPER

Let's dig a little deeper now and see what some other Bible passages have to say about being free through prayer. We'll look at what the Scriptures say, then consider how it applies to our personal lives. There will be a place to record your answers; below that I will give my suggested answers.

If you prefer to continue reading specifically about the Model Prayer, you can turn to Chapter 7 now, and return here later to dig a little deeper.

RUNNING FROM GOD (FROM LUKE 18:9-14)

An eastern newspaper told the story of a woman who was driving home when she noticed a truck tail-gating her. She made a turn, but the truck stayed with her. She sped up, and the truck sped up, too. She ran a red light, and so did the truck!

Panicked, she screeched into a gas station, threw open the door, and ran screaming from her car. The truck driver braked to a stop behind her, and jumped from his vehicle as well. But instead of chasing her, he ran to her car, yanked open the back door, and pulled out a man hiding there! The would-be rapist had been crouched there, unknown to the lady, waiting for his opportunity. The truck driver, from his high vantage point, had seen him. He had chased the woman's car to save her, not to harm her.

When it comes to their relationship with God, many people are like the woman in this incident. They spend their lives running from God, convinced He is out to judge them for their sins, when in reality He is chasing them down to forgive them.

We have learned that in the Model Prayer Jesus said we could be forgiven just for asking. He told us to pray, *"Forgive us our debts."* Since we know He would not have told us to pray a prayer that didn't work, we know God will forgive us when we ask Him to.

But some people are unwilling to ask. It takes humility to admit that you have blown it and need forgiveness. But Jesus told a parable to show that admission of guilt is necessary before we can receive forgiveness. He said:

Two men went up to the temple to pray, one a Pharisee and the other a tax collector. The Pharisee stood up and prayed about himself:

"God, I thank you that I am not like other men—robbers, evildoers, adulterers—or even like this tax collector. I fast twice a week and give a tenth of all I get"

(Luke 18:10-12).

The Pharisee, the first man to pray, was a religious man. The Pharisees were known in Jesus' day for their zeal not only for the Law of Moses, but for the "traditions of the elders"—a list of rules that had developed in addition to the Law of Moses. The Pharisees tried to keep all these rules and looked down on others who didn't.

The Pharisee in this story apparently felt he was doing a pretty good job of keeping all these rules, because his prayer basically consisted of telling God what a good guy he was—especially compared to everyone else. And even more so when compared to this tax collector who was there praying, too.

Tax collectors were at the opposite end of the social and religious spectrum. They were despised by everyone. They were Israelites who worked for the conquering Roman government, and so they were considered traitors. In addition, they had a well-founded reputation for dishonesty. The Roman authorities tended to look the other way if the tax collectors collected a bit more tribute than they were supposed to. It made for motivated collectors. It was a perk for being so hated by their countrymen.

The tax collector who came to the temple that day to pray had apparently had a change of heart. He had perhaps heard Jesus speak, and wanted to get right with God. After all, one of Jesus' twelve disciples was Matthew, a former tax collector. Perhaps there was hope for him as well. Here is what Jesus said about him:

But the tax collector stood at a distance. He would not even look up to heaven, but beat his breast and said,

"God, have mercy on me, a sinner" (Luke 18:13).

This man's prayer was much different than the Pharisee's. He prayed, *"God, have mercy on me, a sinner."* He acknowledged his guilt. He made no excuses, and blamed no one else. He admitted it was all his fault. All he wanted was God's *"mercy."* Guess what? He got it! Jesus said:

"I tell you that this man, rather than the other, went home justified before God. For everyone who exalts himself will be humbled, and he who humbles himself will be exalted" (Luke 18:14).

Jesus said the tax collector went home *"justified before God"*—that is, completely forgiven. What is sobering in this story is that Jesus said the tax collector *"rather than the other"* was forgiven—that is, the Pharisee did not go home forgiven. What was the difference between them? The tax collector was willing to admit he was a sinner who needed forgiveness. The Pharisee was willing to admit no such thing. Forgiveness is ours for the asking. But the asking requires humility. We have to be willing to admit we have blown it and don't measure up on our own merits. Then forgiveness—and freedom from guilt—comes.

The story is told of a king who visited the inhabitants of a prison one day. He talked to a man accused of murder. "I'm innocent," the man said. "They arrested the wrong person."

He talked to another man accused of theft, who told him, "I wasn't stealing the horse . . . just borrowing it."

Another man, accused of treason, said, "I was set up

by my enemies." Every man had a claim of innocence.

Finally, the king stopped at the cell of a man who remained silent.

"Well," the king said, "I suppose you are an innocent victim, too?"

"No, sir, I'm not," the man replied. "I'm guilty and deserve my punishment."

Turning to the warden, the king said, "Right now, release this man—before he corrupts all the fine innocent people in here!" Likewise, our freedom before God does not come from covering up or denying our sin, but from admitting it. God is eager to forgive us. But we have to ask.

IT'S TORTURE (FROM MATTHEW 18:21-35)

A 2004 Readers Digest article, "The Power of Forgiving," told about a study at Hope College in Michigan. In 2001, psychologist Charlotte vanOyen Witvliet, Ph.D., hooked seventy-one college men and women to sensors that would measure their pulse, blood pressure, sweat rates, and muscle tension as they relived past hurts—"lies, insults or betrayals by family members, friends or lovers." They were asked to simulate a grudge, thinking about how those who had wronged them should suffer. As the participants focused on these past slights, their blood pressure rose, heart rate accelerated, muscles tightened, and nervous system activity spiked. In other words, holding a grudge was hard on their health.

When confronted with a crisis situation, the human body releases stress hormones. Their purpose is to stimulate a response that will save us in a dangerous situation. They raise the heart rate, send sugar to our muscles, and quicken our breath and thoughts.

The crisis can be of any kind: a near miss on the freeway, a child's cry for help, a fire alarm—or a simmering feud we rehash in our mind. The hormones don't distinguish between crises. They just go to work.

When the crisis is temporary, the stress hormones do their job and go away—no problem. But when the crisis continues—as when we continue to relive a hurt in our mind—the stress hormones begin to harm us. Too much of the stress hormone cortisol, for example, leads to high blood pressure and elevated blood sugar, hardening of the arteries, and heart disease, according to Bruce McEwen, Ph.D., director of the neuroendocrinology lab at Rockefeller University. It wears down the brain, and leads to cell atrophy and memory loss.

We are harming ourselves when we fail to forgive.

Jesus said this would be the case. He told a parable about a king who decided to collect his debts. He called in one man who owed him *"ten thousand talents"* (Matt. 18:24), which would be the equivalent of millions of dollars today. The man could not pay it, so the king *"ordered that he and his wife and his children and all that he had be sold to repay the debt"* (Matt. 18:25).

In Bible times there were three ways delinquent debtors were dealt with—all of them harsh. The debtor or his family could be forced to work for the lender until the debt was paid. The debtor or his family could be jailed—in the hope that relatives would pay off the debt to free them. Or the debtor and his family could be sold as slaves—to give the lender a chance to recoup at least some of his loss. As I said, all of the ways delinquent debtors were dealt with in Bible times were harsh. There was no Chapter 11 in those days, no filing for bankruptcy.

The king in Jesus' parable chose the third way of dealing with the man who owed him *"ten thousand talents."* He ordered that the man and his family be sold as slaves.

When the man heard this, he fell on his knees and asked for mercy:

"Be patient with me," he begged, *"and I will pay back everything"* (Matt. 18:26b).

Then the king did a remarkable thing:

The servant's master took pity on him, canceled the debt and let him go (Matt. 18:27).

How incredible—the king cancelled the man's debt! The man had asked for time to repay it, but the king went ahead and cancelled it. He forgave the equivalent of millions of dollars of debt.

Imagine if the president of Visa called you up and said, "You know that $3,500 you owe on your credit card? Forget about it. It's cancelled!" Or imagine if the bank called and said, "You know that $185,000 you owe on your house, which you're scheduled to make monthly payments on for the next twenty years? Forget about it. It's cancelled!" Those scenarios take some imagining, don't they? But that is what this king did—he completely wiped out the man's debt.

Who does the king in this story represent? Who does the servant with the impossible debt represent?

The king represents:

_____

The servant with the impossible debt represents:

_____

The merciful king represents God, and the servant with the impossible debt represents you and me. God forgave us our debt of sin, a debt we would never be able to repay ourselves—other than with eternal separation from Him. He forgave us just because we asked Him. He forgave us freely—without asking us to go out and struggle to repay Him somehow.

But that's not the end of Jesus' story. He said the man who had been forgiven his debt went out and *"Found one of his fellow servants who owed him a hundred denarii. He grabbed him and began to choke him. 'Pay back what you owe me!' he demanded"* (Matt. 18:28).

A denarius was a small amount of money compared to a talent. (It took 6,000 denarii just to make up one talent. The first man owed the king 10,000 talents, the equivalent of sixty million denarii. The 100 denarii his fellow servant owed him was microscopic in comparison.) But the man grabbed his fellow servant around the throat and demanded his money:

His fellow servant fell to his knees and begged him, "Be patient with me, and I will pay you back."

But he refused. Instead, he went off and had the man thrown into prison until he could pay the debt (Matt. 18:29-30).

The fellow servant made the same plea of him that he

had made of the king, but he wouldn't listen. He had the man thrown in jail.

When the other servants saw what had happened, they were greatly distressed and went and told their master everything that had happened.

Then the master called the servant in. "You wicked servant," he said, "I canceled all that debt of yours because you begged me to. Shouldn't you have had mercy on your fellow servant just as I had on you?" In anger his master turned him over to the jailers to be tortured, until he should pay back all he owed.

This is how my heavenly Father will treat each of you unless you forgive your brother from your heart (Matt. 18:31-35, emphasis added).

The man the king had forgiven a great amount would not forgive his fellow servant a relatively small amount. The king was furious when he heard. The man was arrested and thrown into jail "to be tortured." Jesus said the Heavenly Father will do the same to us if we don't forgive.

We learned earlier in the chapter that when God says He won't forgive us if we don't forgive others, He is not referring to forgiveness in an eternal sense. He has promised we would be eternally saved if we put our faith in Jesus, and He won't contradict Himself (John 5:24, Acts 16:31, Rom. 10:9-10, Eph. 2:8-9). He is referring to forgiveness in an experiential sense. We won't experience the blessings that are ours because of His forgiveness of us if we fail to forgive others. We will, in fact, be *"tortured"* (Matt. 18:34).

As we've seen, modern research has revealed what

some of the torture consists of: accelerated heart rates, high blood pressure, heart disease, brain cell atrophy, memory loss, and so on. We inflict physical, mental, and emotional stress on ourselves when we refuse to forgive. We are our own torturers.

It is costly to hold a grudge. Peter Johnson, in USA Today, wrote about the legendary feud between the Hatfields and the McCoys. No one's sure how it got started, perhaps over the Civil War (the McCoys sympathized with the Union, while the Hatfields sympathized with the South), or perhaps over an accusation that the Hatfields were stealing hogs. Whatever the cause, the two families fought each other for years across the Kentucky border. It lasted until May 1976, when Jim McCoy and Willis Hatfield—the last survivors of the original families—shook hands at a public ceremony dedicating a monument to the victims of the feud. When McCoy himself died in 1984 (at the age of ninety-nine), his burial was handled by the Hatfield Funeral Home in Toler, KY.

Peace at last, but peace too late: as many as 100 men, women, and children died in the fighting. It is costly to hold a grudge.

On the other hand, forgiveness sets us free, as the story of Holland's Corrie ten Boom demonstrates. Corrie was arrested along with her family for hiding Jews from the Nazis during World War II. She was sent with her sister to a concentration camp, where they experienced numerous horrors, and where her sister died. After the war, Corrie had a speaking ministry, telling of the miraculous ways God had seen her through the suffering. One evening, at a service, she saw one of the guards from the concentration camp! In her book *The Hiding Place* she recounts what happened:

It was at a church service in Munich that I saw him, the former S.S. man who had stood guard at the shower room door in the processing center at Ravensbruck . . . And suddenly it was all there—the roomful of mocking men, the heaps of clothing, Betsie's pain-blanched face.

He came up to me as the church was emptying, beaming and bowing.

"How grateful I am for your message, Fraulein," he said. "To think that, as you say, He has washed my sins away!"

His hand thrust out to shake mine. And I, who had preached so often to the people in Bloemendaal the need to forgive, kept my hand at my side.

. . . I tried to smile, I struggled to raise my hand. I could not. I felt nothing, not the slightest spark of warmth or charity. And so again I breathed a silent prayer. Jesus, I cannot forgive him. Give me Your forgiveness.

As I took his hand the most incredible thing happened. From my shoulder along my arm and through my hand a current seemed to pass from me to him, while into my heart sprang a love for this stranger that almost overwhelmed me.

And so I discovered that it is not on our forgiveness any more than on our goodness that the world's healing hinges, but on His. When He tells us to love our enemies, He gives, along with the command, the love itself.

When Corrie chose to forgive, God's love came on the scene and empowered her to do it. She was set free of the bitterness she felt for the former guard. Forgiveness set her free.

Is there someone you need to forgive? A parent who abused you? A son or daughter who spurned your love? A criminal who hurt you? A pastor or church who betrayed your trust?

"But they don't deserve it." You are right. But we didn't deserve the forgiveness God gave us. "But they shouldn't get away with it." You are right. But remember, it is God's job to bring the consequences (Rom. 12:19). "I don't know if I can. It hurts too much." You can—as an act of your will. When we choose to obey like Corrie did, we'll be the ones set free.

Read the following verses from Proverbs. Write down what they teach about the privilege of forgiveness:

A man's wisdom gives him patience; it is to his glory to overlook an offense (Prov. 19:11).

_____

_____

(Forgiving is a wise and glorious act. It is one of the godliest things we can ever do.)

It is to a man's honor to avoid strife, but every fool is quick to quarrel (Prov. 20:3).

_____

_____

(Anybody can hold a grudge. It is to our credit when we can forgive.)

Better a patient man than a warrior, a man who controls his temper than one who takes a city (Prov. 16:32).

_____

_____

(Forgiveness releases great spiritual power.)

Chapter 7

BEING LED THROUGH PRAYER

I ONCE HAD THE SAD duty of ministering at a funeral for a twelve-year-old boy named Nick. A car struck the bike he was riding, and he was killed. I had baptized Nick a few years earlier, so I knew that he was with the Lord, but still it was a tragic, heart-breaking time for his family.

But God delivered a gracious message to the family in the midst of it all in a surprising way. It seems that Nick for some reason, about a week before the accident, had begun wearing his mom's jacket around. After his death, two quarters were found in the pockets of this jacket. One was dated 1982, the year of Nick's birth. The other was dated 1994, the year of his death. This may have seemed a coincidence to some, but to the family it was a profound message. They took it as a word from heaven—that God was aware of all the details of this tragedy, that their son's life was in His hands, and that somehow some good purpose would come of it.

God is still able to communicate with His people, even in the darkest of times. One of the reasons God communicates with us is to guide us. He communicated with Nick's family to guide them through their tragedy. He communicates with all of us to guide us through the challenges and difficulties of life.

In the next line of the Model Prayer, in the first half of verse 13, Jesus told us to pray for God's guidance:

And lead us not into temptation (Matt 6:13a).

124

Specifically, He was telling us to pray for guidance through "temptation"—for guidance to victory over sin. Generally, I believe, He was inviting us to pray for guidance in all areas of life, because all areas of life present us with choices and challenges (i.e., "*temptations*").

*Teach me your way, O LORD; **lead me** in a straight path because of my oppressors* (Ps. 27:11, emphasis added).

We can ask God for guidance. Remember, Jesus would not have told us to pray a prayer that didn't work. We can ask God for guidance, and expect an answer.

But how will the guidance come? You may have noticed, when you've asked the Lord to lead you in some area of life, that He's never responded with a neon sign flashing the answer in the sky. He probably hasn't sent you a text message with your answer. You've probably never heard an audible voice.

There are three basic ways God guides His people, when we ask Him to. He is certainly not limited to these ways, but these are the most basic and common ways we experience his guidance. Let's look at them.

WHEN WE ASK GOD FOR GUIDANCE, HE DIRECTS US THROUGH HIS WRITTEN WORD, THE BIBLE.

The Bible is the most authoritative form of guidance we can receive. If the Bible tells us to do one thing, and some other form of so-called guidance tells us to do something else, the Bible always trumps the other voice—be it the voice of a pastor, a church, or even an angel.

"Even an *angel?*" you might ask. Yes, even an angel, as the Apostle Paul warned in Galatians 1:8:

*"But even if we or an **angel** from heaven should preach a gospel other than the one we preached to you, let him be eternally condemned!"* (emphasis added).

Some modern cults and false religions, leading millions astray, never would have gotten started if their leaders had obeyed this verse and ignored the so-called angels who visited them with a different "gospel."

The written Word of God is the most authoritative form of guidance we can receive. Jesus said the Word of God is more reliable than the rising of the sun:

"Heaven and earth will pass away, but my words will never pass away" (Matt. 24:35).

Jesus said the Word of God will judge us someday: *"the word I spoke is what will judge him at the last day"* (John 12:48b, NASB). Jesus Himself received His direction from the written Word of God. Look at His responses when the devil tempted Him:

Then Jesus was led by the Spirit into the desert to be tempted by the devil. After fasting forty days and forty nights, he was hungry. The tempter came to him and said, "If you are the Son of God, tell these stones to become bread."

Jesus answered, "It is written: *'Man does not live on* bread alone, but on every word that comes from the mouth of God.'"

Then the devil took him to the holy city and had him stand on the highest point of the temple. "If you are the Son of God," he said, "throw yourself down. For it is written: 'He will command his angels concerning you, and they will lift you up in their hands, so that you will not strike your foot against a stone.'"

Jesus answered him, "It is also written: 'Do not put the Lord your God to the test.'"

Again, the devil took him to a very high mountain and showed him all the kingdoms of the world and their splendor. "All this I will give you," he said, "if you will bow down and worship me."

Jesus said to him, "Away from me, Satan! **For it is written:** 'Worship the Lord your God, and serve him only.'"

Then the devil left him, and angels came and attended him (Matt. 4:2-11, emphasis added).

Notice that Jesus responded to every temptation with a quote from the written Word of God (all from the Old Testament book Deuteronomy: respectively, 8:3, 6:16, 6:13). He responded each time with the phrase, "It is written." When Jesus needed guidance, the first place He looked was the Bible.

Jesus was the Son of God. He had lived for eternity in heaven. As He walked the earth, He had unbroken communication with His Heavenly Father (John 5:20). All the angels were at His disposal (Matt. 26:53). You might think He would have some secret spiritual weapon to rely on when the devil tempted Him, but He relied on the same Book at your disposal!

When we ask God for guidance, the first place we should look for it is in His Word. We should ask, "What does the Bible say about this decision I'm facing?" God will bring to mind Scriptures we've read, sermons we've heard, or promises we've memorized. As we're faithful to read our Bible daily, we'll be surprised how often we find it addressing the very issues we're facing. The psalmist wrote: *"Your word is a lamp to my feet and a light for my path"* (Ps. 119:105). The written Word will be our guide through this dark world.

A Chicago bus driver was making his stops. His bus was filled with passengers—shoppers, people going home from work, teenagers. At the Clark and Webster stop, two men and a woman got on. The seasoned bus driver immediately called out, "Everybody, watch your valuables. Pickpockets on board!" All eyes fixed on the newcomers, as women clutched their purses, and men guarded their wallets. The pickpockets didn't break stride as they promptly exited through the middle doors. Their plans had been spoiled by the driver's warning.

The Bible is like that bus driver, given to conduct us safely on our journey through life. When you ask God for guidance, tune your ear first to the warnings and wisdom in His written Word.

That's one of the basic ways God guides His people. Let's look at the second one.

WHEN WE ASK GOD FOR GUIDANCE, HE DIRECTS US THROUGH HIS HOLY SPIRIT.

Did you know that Jesus promised that the Holy Spirit, the Third Person of the Trinity, would talk to you? Jesus said of Him:

*"But when he, the Spirit of truth, comes, **he will guide you** into all truth. He will not speak on His own; **he will speak** only what he hears, and **he will tell you** what is yet to come"* (John 16:13, emphasis added).

Jesus was telling the disciples that the Holy Spirit was going to come to the church after Jesus returned to heaven. This happened on the Day of Pentecost (see Acts 2). Jesus said the Holy Spirit would *"guide"* the church, and that he would do it by *talking to them:*

- *"He will speak"*
- *"He will tell"*

Jesus promised that the Holy Spirit would *"guide"* us, and that He would do it by *talking* to us. Remarkable! When we ask God to guide us, the second basic way He does it is through His Spirit.

How do we learn to hear the voice of the Holy Spirit, then? A complete answer to that question would require its own book. But here are a few lessons I have learned about hearing from the Holy Spirit:

First, He speaks to us with varying degrees of intensity.

Often He will speak to us and we won't even be aware of it—we'll be hearing Him subconsciously. This is the lowest degree of intensity with which He will speak to us. We will have a good idea, or make a decision that works out. Or it will come to our mind to pray for someone. We'll decide to help out in a ministry at church, which turns out to be a big blessing to others as well as to ourselves. The Holy Spirit led us in all these ways without us being aware of it.

He speaks to us through our conscience, a higher degree of intensity than when we hear from Him subconsciously. People don't talk about the conscience much anymore in our society, but the conscience is one of the stars God uses to navigate us through life. Paul wrote the young minister Timothy and encouraged him to keep *"faith and a **good conscience,** which some have rejected and suffered shipwreck in regard to their faith"* (1 Tim. 1:19, NASB, emphasis added). If we reject a *"good conscience,"* we can get off course and suffer *"shipwreck."*

Have you asked the Lord for guidance? In your heart do you already know the morally right thing to do? The Holy Spirit is using your conscience to guide you.

I should add, however, that the conscience is not a perfect guide. Your conscience itself is *not* the Holy Spirit, but a tool in your soul or spirit that He uses. Some people's consciences are *over-sensitive*—that is, they feel bad for things they shouldn't feel bad about. Or they overreact to a wrong they've done. Judas is an example of the latter. When he betrayed Jesus, he certainly should have felt remorse. However, his conscience drove him too far, leading him to commit suicide, thus compounding the evil. The Lord certainly would have forgiven him if he had come to him instead. What a tragedy.

Other people have what the Bible calls a *seared* conscience (see 1 Timothy 4:2)—a conscience that has grown callous and doesn't feel the pain it should feel anymore. Back in my bar-hopping days, the first drink I swallowed burned going down. The second one burned a little, too. But before long they went down like water. My throat was seared to the sensation. That's what happens to a conscience that is long ignored. Sin or hypocrisy that may have bothered it at first doesn't anymore.

The conscience is not a perfect guide. It can be *over-sensitive* or *seared*. But it is a tool the Holy Spirit uses to speak to us. That is why it is important that we do our best to maintain a good conscience.

The Holy Spirit will also speak to us through a sense of knowing, another degree of intensity with which He speaks to us. The Apostle John wrote, *"But you have an anointing from the Holy One, and all of you **know** the truth"* (1 John 2:20, emphasis added). The *"anointing"* refers to the presence of the Holy Spirit in us; John says that through that presence we will come to *"**know** the truth."* That is, we will have a *sense of knowing* about the way we should go. We may not have it at first, but eventually it will come.

He speaks to us with words. This is probably the highest degree of intensity with which God speaks to us. Of course, He also uses words when He speaks to us in the above ways. But there is a communication from the Lord where the words are more direct, almost audible.

One day, when I was a new Christian, I was jogging in my neighborhood when a man in a wheelchair asked me for some money. I gave him some, but saw him later in the grocery store buying a load of beer. I was pretty angry at being taken advantage of.

A Saturday rolled around, and I was looking forward to going to church the next day, when the thought came to me that I should invite Jim (the man's name). But then I thought, *No way, I don't want to invite a lying drunk to church with me.*

Then I heard the words: "But someone invited you."

The words seemed to "go off" inside of me. They were authoritative, but not condemning. They were filled with love. And they were *true*. Someone *had* invited me, and it had changed my life.

I drove to Jim's apartment and invited him. He agreed, and I picked him up the next morning. He was the first person to respond to the invitation to accept Jesus. He became a new person. He quit drinking, joined the church, and became a personal friend. When he moved back home a couple years later, he was still living for the Lord.

His story is one of my best memories, and it's because of the words: "But someone invited you."

The Holy Spirit speaks to us with varying degrees of intensity: subconsciously, through our conscience, through a sense of knowing, and through words.

A second lesson I've learned about hearing from the Holy Spirit:

He speaks to different people in different ways.

I used to wonder if there was something wrong with me when God wouldn't speak to me in the same way He spoke to others—for example, through dreams or visions. (The main way I hear from the Holy Spirit is by meditating on Scripture: taking a promise or instruction or truth, and asking God, "What difference does this Scripture make in my life? How does it change my life?") I've come to realize that God made us all unique, and enjoys speaking to us in different ways. So don't worry if your experience doesn't quite match up with someone else's. That's normal.

The third lesson I've learned about hearing from the Holy Spirit:

We hear Him better the closer we get to Him.

The Bible says that God speaks in _"a gentle whisper"_ (1 Kings 19:12). You have to draw close to someone to hear Him whisper.

You also have to be quiet. You have to tune out the other noise and listen intently to the whisperer.

Before refrigerators came along, people preserved their food in icehouses. An icehouse was a building with thick walls, no windows, and a tightly fitted door. In the winter large blocks of ice were cut from frozen lakes or streams, hauled to the icehouse, and covered with sawdust. Sometimes the ice in the icehouses would last into summer. One man lost a valuable watch while working inside one of these icehouses. He looked for it, raking through the sawdust, but couldn't find it. Other workers looked, but they had no luck either.

A small boy volunteered to give it a try. He went into the icehouse during the noon hour, and a little while later emerged with the watch. "How did you find it?" the men asked.

"I closed the door. Laid down in the sawdust, and kept very still. Soon I heard the watch ticking."

None of the men heard the watch because they didn't take the time to get quiet first.

It's the same way when it comes to hearing from the Holy Spirit. He is speaking to us, but it's a whisper. We have to draw close to Him, quiet ourselves, and listen.

Learning to hear from the Holy Spirit is a life-long

study, but understanding these principles will get you off to a good start: God speaks to us with varying degrees of intensity. God speaks to different people in different ways. The closer we get to God, the better we hear him.

So far in this chapter, we have seen that when we ask God for guidance, He directs us through His Word. He directs us through His Spirit. Let's look at one more basic way God guides His people when we ask Him to.

WHEN WE ASK GOD FOR GUIDANCE, HE DIRECTS THROUGH HIS PROVIDENCE—THAT IS, HE EITHER PROVIDES A WAY OR HE DOESN'T.

We see this in the Apostle Paul's ministry. On his second missionary journey, as he was taking the Gospel to the world, there was a point in his ministry when he wanted to head east but the Holy Spirit wouldn't let him.

Paul and his companions traveled throughout the region of Phrygia and Galatia, having been kept by the Holy Spirit from preaching the word in the province of Asia. When they came to the border of Mysia, they tried to enter Bithynia, but the Spirit of Jesus would not allow them to (Acts 16:6-7).

Paul and his companions were "kept by the Holy Spirit from preaching the word in province of Asia." We're not told how the Holy Spirit prevented them from turning east, whether it was by circumstances, a vision, or their own reasoning. We're just told "the Spirit of Jesus would not allow them to."

For some reason, the door was closed. But another

During the night Paul had a vision of a man of Macedonia standing and begging him, "Come over to Macedonia and help us." After Paul had seen the vision, we got ready at once to leave for Macedonia, concluding that God had called us to preach the gospel to them (Acts 16:9-10).

God closed the door to the east for them. But he opened one to the west. A *"man of Macedonia"* appeared to Paul in a vision and asked him to come preach the Gospel to them. Paul obeyed the vision and ended up taking the Gospel into the heart of Europe.

The point is, Paul received guidance for his mission by God's provision. Somehow God closed a door to the east. But He opened one to the west. Paul followed the provision.

When we ask God for guidance, He will often use His providence to direct us—by either providing a way or not. You may ask God if you should change jobs, for example. But as you begin to investigate new opportunities, you find no openings, or no openings that pay enough. That may be God's way of saying, "No, it's not my will for you to change jobs." Or you might be praying about whether you should help with the teenagers at church or the preschoolers. Which group do you prefer to be around? Which group touches your heart more? Those positive feelings may be God's way of guiding you—His provision.

We should keep in mind, however, that just because God opens a door and directs us down a path, that doesn't mean that we won't have problems. When Paul crossed over to help the man in Macedonia, it wasn't long before he was beaten and thrown in jail! And he wrote in another place: *"A great door for effective work has opened to me, and there are many who oppose me"* (1 Cor. 16:9). Opposition came with the open doors for Paul. God will guide us by His provision and by open doors, but there will still be obstacles to overcome. But if we're in His will, He will give us victory over every situation. Paul also wrote: *"But thanks be to God, who* ***always leads us in triumph in Christ,*** *and manifests through us the sweet aroma of the knowledge of Him in every place"* (2 Cor. 2:14, NASB, emphasis added).

Do you need guidance? Sure, consult other people. Sure, think it through thoroughly yourself. But don't forget to ask God what you should do! Jesus promised He would guide us.

SUMMARY

God still guides His people. Jesus said that we should pray for guidance: *"And* ***lead us*** *not into temptation"* (emphasis added). He wouldn't have told us to pray a prayer that didn't work. When we pray for guidance, God directs us through his written Word, through His Spirit, and through His provision.

DIGGING DEEPER

Let's dig a little deeper now and see what some other Bible passages have to say about being led through prayer. We'll look at what the Scriptures say, then consider how it applies to our personal lives. There will be a place to record your answers; below that I will give my suggested answers.

If you prefer to continue reading specifically about the Model Prayer, you can turn to Chapter 8 now, and return here later to dig a little deeper.

THE SOUND OF HIS VOICE (FROM 1 KINGS 19:1-18)

In the 1990s *The Associated Press* carried the story of a group of people who traveled from Texas to Louisiana—naked! There were twenty of them, all related, traveling from the small town of Floydada, in the Texas Panhandle. They started out in several cars, but by the time they reached Vinton, Louisiana, they were all in one 1990 Pontiac Grand Am. When they attracted the attention of police in Vinton, they tried to flee. They sped down Vinton's main street, but hit a tree at a baseball park at the end of town. Fifteen adults (as old as sixty-three) piled out of the car, and five children (as young as one) came out of the trunk. And they were all completely naked.

Why were they naked? They said they were following God's instructions. "The Lord told them to get rid of all their belongings and go to Louisiana," Vinton's Police Chief Dennis Drouillard explained. "So they got rid of all their clothes and pocketbooks and wallets and identification and the license plate off their car and came to our gorgeous state."

Their car was totaled when they hit the tree, but there were no serious injuries. The driver was booked on various charges, and the others were released to a nearby church.

When it comes to receiving guidance from God, it is

137

obvious that we can be misled. We can think God is telling us to do something, but we're really just following our own desires, someone else's, or even the devil's.

One reason we make mistakes when it comes to receiving guidance from God is that we don't know the sound of His voice. We have not learned to recognize when God is speaking to us. What does His voice sound like? How will it make us feel when we hear it? What will it tell us to do? We need to know these things to receive guidance from Him.

The prophet Elijah was given a lesson once in recognizing the sound of God's voice, a lesson we can learn from. Right after his greatest victory—right after God had answered from heaven and burned up his sacrifice in full view of all the people—Elijah had his greatest failure. The idolatrous Queen Jezebel sent word that she was going to kill him, and Elijah ran. Normal fear had something to do with it, but discouragement was also a factor. After the miracle of the fire from heaven, Elijah thought that surely revival would follow and his nation would turn to God. But it didn't happen. The idol-worshiping queen was still in power, and seeking his life. Elijah ran.

There's a side lesson for us in Elijah's experience here: After a victory, expect a counter-attack. The enemy doesn't like losing ground to us. He will send a temptation, a discouragement, or a trial to strike back. Don't let your guard down.

Elijah journeyed forty days into the desert. He came to Mount Sinai, where God had given the Ten Commandments to Moses, and went into a cave to spend the night. The Bible says:

And the word of the LORD came to him: "What are you doing here, Elijah?"

He replied, "I have been very zealous for the LORD God Almighty. The Israelites have rejected your covenant, broken down your altars, and put your prophets to death with the sword. I am the only one left, and now they are trying to kill me too" (1 Kings 19:9b-10).

Can you hear his discouragement? Elijah thinks he's the only true believer left, and that his ministry has failed.

The LORD said, "Go out and stand on the mountain in the presence of the LORD, for the LORD is about to pass by" (1 Kings 19:11a).

God tells Elijah to go outside and get ready to hear a word from Him. Watch what happens:

Then a great and powerful wind tore the mountains apart and shattered the rocks before the LORD, but the LORD was not in the wind. After the wind there was an earthquake, but the LORD was not in the earthquake. After the earthquake came a fire, but the LORD was not in the fire. And after the fire came a gentle whisper. When Elijah heard it, he pulled his cloak over his face and went out and stood at the mouth of the cave.

Then a voice said to him, "What are you doing here, Elijah?" (1 Kings 19:11b-13).

Elijah experienced three powerful natural phenomena in which he did not find God's presence or hear His voice. What were the three natural phenomena?

_____

_____

_____

(A powerful wind (11), an earthquake (11), and a fire (12))

After the three powerful natural phenomena, Elijah did hear God's voice. In what manner did God's voice come to him?

_____

(In a gentle whisper 12-13)

Elijah experienced three powerful natural phenomena—a strong wind, an earthquake, and fire—in which he did not hear God's voice. But then *"came a gentle whisper"* (12), and Elijah in reverence pulled *"his cloak over his face"* (13)—because it was in the *"gentle whisper"* (the *"still small voice,"* as the King James Version translates it) that Elijah did hear God's voice.

What I want you to notice is that Elijah did not hear God's voice in the spectacular displays of wind, fire, and earthquake—where he seems to have been looking for it—but in a gentle whisper.

And what did the gentle whisper tell Elijah?

The LORD said to him, "Go back the way you came, and go to the
Desert of Damascus. When you get there, anoint Hazael king over
Aram. Also, anoint Jehu son of Nimshi king over Israel, and anoint Elisha son of Shaphat from Abel Meholah to succeed you as prophet" (1 Kings 19:15-16).

The gentle whisper told Elijah to get back to doing what a prophet is supposed to be doing: anoint a new king over a foreign country, as well as a new king over Israel; and anoint a prophet to follow in Elijah's footsteps. In other words, God gives him a fresh start, re-commissions him. He basically tells him to stop wallowing in self-pity and get back to living his life. Then He has even better news for Elijah:

Yet I reserve seven thousand in Israel—all whose knees have not bowed down to Baal and all whose mouths have not kissed him (1 Kings 19:18).

In other words, "Elijah, you're far from the last true believer left. There are plenty of people still faithful to me in Israel. Your ministry has not been without impact." The gentle whisper had good news for Elijah.

Elijah did not find God's voice in the spectacular displays of wind, fire, and earthquake, and neither will we. We will find it in the gentle whisper.

It is vitally important that we learn to recognize the sound of God's voice, or we can be terribly misled.

You may remember hearing about the "Uganda Doomsday Cult." Their official name was a mouthful: The Movement for the Restoration of the Ten Commandments of God. In the spring of 2000, they made headlines—because they decided to kill their followers.

The group was organized around a number of strict rules. The followers were told to give all their belongings to the group. They were forbidden to speak with each other except in religious services (because, one of their rules said, "conversations lead many into telling lies about their neighbors"). Smoking and drinking were forbidden, and AIDS was considered God's punishment for drinking beer. Strict fasting and prayer were musts.

In spite of the stringent rules—or perhaps because of them—the cult had hundreds of followers, with branches stretching into Tanzania and Rwanda.

The leaders of the group not only drew up a list of tough requirements, they also made the mistake of prophesying that the world would end before January 1, 2000. When it didn't, they pushed back the forecast until the next January—but the damage had been done. Members began to lose confidence and to demand their money back.

So the leaders decided to get rid of them. They gathered them in the chapel at their main compound, nailed shut the doors and windows, and in an act of incomprehensible evil set the building on fire. Over 500 died. Then more bodies were found in mass graves at the cult's other compounds. Some had been stabbed, some strangled. Many were children. The death toll kept increasing until it surpassed the 913 who died in the 1978 Jonestown tragedy in Guyana, the previous record for deaths in a modern-day cult-related massacre.

Why did these poor people fall to this terrible tragedy? They did not know the sound of their Heavenly Father's voice. When leaders bullied, controlled, and used them in God's name, they didn't know any better. They didn't know the gentle whisper.

One of the ways to recognize the gentle whisper is by the effect it has on us. Consider again the effect God's word had on Elijah:

- It encouraged Elijah to consider his ways. God

asked him, *"What are you doing here, Elijah?"* (1 Kings 19:9). God's word will correct us without condemning us.

- It gave Elijah new direction. God told him to go anoint two men as kings over their respective lands, and another man as a prophet to succeed Elijah. God's word will give us light for our path, and show us the next step to take.

- It gave Elijah hope. *"Yet I reserve seven thousand in Israel . . . whose knees have not bowed down to Baal"* (1 Kings 19:18). God revealed to Elijah that the situation was not as bad as he thought: God was in control. God's word will give us hope as well—the confidence that God is going to work things out for us if we continue to follow Him.

It is possible to be misled when it comes to receiving guidance from God. Overzealous preachers have been misled. Terrorists who blow up others in God's name are obviously misled. The naïve who follow controlling cults are misled. We will protect ourselves against deception if we'll learn to recognize the sound of God's voice—the gentle whisper that corrects, directs, and gives us hope.

In the lines below, write down three messages you believe God is giving you for your life, three things He is leading you to do:

_____

_____

_____

Now for each message, ask, "Does this message come to me in the gentle whisper of a loving Heavenly

Father?" Also ask, "Will obeying this message have a positive, godly effect on my life, like God's message to Elijah had on his life?" If the message does not pass both these tests, draw a line through it and forget about it. If it does pass the test, put a star by it—in all likelihood you are experiencing the Lord's guidance here.

THINKING FOR YOURSELF (FROM ACTS 17:1-4)

If you've raised children, then you know that the younger they are the more guidance they need. Infants, toddlers, and preschoolers need almost constant guidance. The parent decides what they will wear, eat, play with, and so on. The parent gives constant warnings: "Don't put that in your mouth." "Don't touch! It's hot." The parent is continually teaching: "Wear your coat and hat when it's cold outside." "Wash your hands before eating."

As the children grow, their need for guidance decreases. By the time they are leaving elementary school, we hope they no longer need to be told to brush their teeth or put on clean underwear. As they progress through their teen years, we gradually give them more and more freedom as they prove to be responsible, even to the point of giving them a driver's license. They still need guidance, probably lots of correction, but our aim is to teach them how to make good decisions on their own.

And then they become adults, running their own lives. They will still, if they are smart, come to us parents for guidance from time to time on issues they're facing—after all, we've been there, done that— but the decision

144

will be theirs. This is how things were designed to be.

This is how things were designed to be spiritually as well. This surprises some people, but God doesn't want to run your life and make all your decisions for you. He doesn't want to have to give you constant guidance. He wants you to mature to where you can make many, even most, of your decisions for yourself—because you already know right from wrong. He's there to give guidance when you need it, but the majority of the day-to-day decisions He entrusts to you. He made you in His image, with the ability to think and make decisions for yourself. He enjoys letting you do it.

As new Christians, we need constant guidance. As newborn spiritual babies (1 Peter 2:2), we need to learn what is right and wrong in God's eyes, what spiritual food we should eat, what companions we should have, and what tasks we should be doing to serve God. It is a whole new world to us, and we need direction.

But as we grow spiritually, the need for direction should decrease. We shouldn't need daily guidance to remind us to read the Bible, for example. We should have developed that commitment and habit in our life already. We should not need a special leading from the Holy Spirit to tell us to go to church, tell the truth, and stay morally pure. We should already know God's will in these matters.

The point is, as we grow spiritually, we don't need to pray for guidance in everything. In a sense, God has already given us guidance about many of the things we face—by the principles we've learned from His Word and the experiences He's allowed us to have. He has been forming *"the mind of Christ"* (1 Cor. 2:16) in us, and wants us to think for ourselves.

We see this in the Apostle Paul's life. Paul is the apostle most responsible for taking the Gospel to the Gentile world. His missionary journeys took him all the way from Jerusalem to Rome. The following passage summarizes the strategy Paul used to reach people with the Gospel. Read it and write down the "custom" (2) Paul followed as he took the Gospel to a new area.

When they had passed through Amphipolis and Apollonia, they came to Thessalonica, where there was a Jewish synagogue. As his custom was, Paul went into the synagogue, and on three Sabbath days he reasoned with them from the Scriptures, explaining and proving that the Christ had to suffer and rise from the dead. "This Jesus I am proclaiming to you is the Christ," he said. Some of the Jews were persuaded and joined Paul and Silas, as did a large number of God-fearing Greeks and not a few prominent women (Acts 17:1-4).

Paul's custom when he visited a new area:

_____

(Paul's custom was to go into the synagogue on the Sabbath and preach the Gospel from the Scriptures (2))

Paul's *"custom"* (2) when he visited a new city was to go to the synagogue on the day of worship and preach Jesus from the Scriptures. It was not something he needed guidance to do. He did it every time he could. Why? Because it made sense.

Paul's custom actually included more than we find in verse 2. If we look at the whole passage, we'll see that Paul's custom actually included six things:

1. Paul visited cities. In this passage, he is visiting

Thessalonica (1), which was the capital of the province of Macedonia and had a population of more than 200,000 people. Paul went there for the same reason he visited the other cities (Philippi, Athens, Corinth, Ephesus, Rome): that's where most of the people were. Paul wanted to reach all people, not just city dwellers, but he trusted that the Word would spread from the cities to the regions beyond, and it did (see Acts 19:10).

Paul didn't have to pray about taking the Gospel to cities every time. It was the custom he had developed. It made sense.

2. As mentioned, Paul went into the synagogue—which was the Jewish equivalent of the local church. Paul went to the synagogue because this is where he would find people interested in spiritual things. The Jewish people would be there, as well as the "God-fearers" (4)—non-Jewish people who had not become full-fledged converts to Judaism, but were believers in the God of the Jews, and were waiting for His promised Messiah.

Paul knew he would find people interested in the Gospel at the synagogue. It made sense to go there.

3. As mentioned, he went to the synagogue on the Sabbath. The Sabbath was when people worshiped. It made sense to go then.

4. As mentioned, he spoke to the gathered worshipers from the Scriptures. This refers to the Old Testament books on hand, which contained the prophecies concerning the Messiah, and which both the Jews and God-fearers accepted as the Word of God.

5. He preached Jesus: *"This Jesus I am proclaiming to you is the Christ"* (3). He didn't preach his own philosophy, politics, or the latest fads of culture. His

147

message was about Jesus Christ.

6. He called for a decision: *"Some of the Jews were persuaded and joined Paul and Silas, as did a large number of God-fearing Greeks and not a few prominent women"* (4).

These six customs of Paul—the strategy he used in spreading the Gospel—were not matters he had to pray about everywhere he went. He knew they worked and were God's will. He knew they made sense. Perhaps he had prayed about them at first. Perhaps he had learned from experience that they worked. Or perhaps it had just been a matter of logic (of course, you'll reach more people in a city; of course, you'll find the people interested in spiritual matters at the synagogue).

The point is the Lord did not have to guide Paul on these matters every time. Paul had matured to the point that he could make these decisions himself. Paul was open to new direction (as we saw earlier in the chapter, when Paul allowed a dream from the Lord to redirect his traveling plans from the east to the west), but he also felt free to think for himself.

Have you been hesitating to take action because you are waiting on God for some specific guidance? Of course, many times that's the course we should take. But many times the Lord is waiting for us to think for ourselves.

Missionary Marti Ensign invited some African pastors to the United States for a meeting. During some free time, they wanted to go shopping. Marti gave them her number in case they ran into a difficulty or got lost. Sure enough, in less than an hour the phone rang. "I am lost," the African said.

Marti told him to put the phone down, go and find out

the names of the two streets at the corner, come back and tell her, and she'd come get him.

In a few minutes his voice came back over the line: "I am at the corner of 'Walk' and 'Don't walk.'"

Have you ever felt like that in life, stuck at a crossroads, not sure which way to go? It may be that God has already shown you—by what He's taught you through His Word and your experiences. Perhaps He is waiting on you to make the decision. You can think for yourself.

What is one custom or practice God has taught you, which doesn't require a prayer for guidance each time?

_____

_____

MAKING PROGRESS (FROM THE BOOK OF JONAH)

A woman was driving through the Cascade Mountains in Oregon when she ran into a snowstorm. She became frightened, and was happy to see a snowplow up ahead. She pulled in behind it and began to follow it.

The snowplow turned this way and that, clearing the snow ahead. The woman just relaxed and followed. At times the heavy snowfall threatened to cut off her vision, but she stayed right on the tail of the snowplow.

Finally, the snowplow stopped. The driver came back to her and asked, "Lady, where are you going?"

"I'm on my way to central Oregon," she said.

"You won't get there following me. I'm plowing this parking lot," he said.

Have you ever felt like that lady? You've been

149

journeying down the road of life, turning this way and that, but not really making much progress? We have probably all felt that way at one time or another.

Sometimes in life it only *seems* like we're not making progress, while in reality God is busy working behind the scenes, moving His plan for our life forward. We just have to be patient. At other times we really are *not* making progress. Like the lady in the snowstorm, we have gotten off course somewhere. God's plan for our life is not moving forward.

This usually happens when we have failed to follow God's leading at some point. We may have failed to do one of the basic things all Christians are called to do, like forgiving others, attending church, or being thankful. Or we may have missed God's leading in regard to His unique plan for our life. We may be trying to be a pastor when He's called us to be a stockbroker—or vice versa. Either way, we have failed to follow God's leading in some area of our life, and have stopped making progress.

This happened to the prophet Jonah. God gave him some specific instructions:

Go to the great city of Nineveh and preach against it, because its wickedness has come up before me (Jonah 1:2).

But Jonah did the exact opposite:

But Jonah ran away from the LORD and headed for Tarshish. He went down to Joppa, where he found a ship bound for that port. After paying the fare, he went aboard and sailed for Tarshish to flee from the LORD (Jonah 1:3).

Jonah failed to follow God's leading for his life. God told him to go to Nineveh, but Jonah took a boat to Tarshish instead. He didn't want to preach to the city of Nineveh, because it was the capital of Assyria, his nation Israel's enemy.

Because Jonah failed to follow God's leading, his life went into a tailspin. A great storm came on the ship he was in, threatening to sink it. Jonah knew the storm had come because of him. He admitted it to the sailors, who threw him overboard—and the storm stopped.

But the LORD provided a great fish to swallow Jonah, and Jonah was inside the fish three days and three nights (Jonah 1:17).

Inside the fish Jonah cried for mercy, and God heard him:

And the LORD commanded the fish, and it vomited Jonah onto dry land (Jonah 2:10).

So Jonah was given a second chance:

Then the word of the LORD came to Jonah a second time: "Go to the great city of Nineveh and proclaim to it the message I give you" (Jonah 3:1-2).

Notice that God's word to Jonah has not changed. Before he fled in the ship, God's word to him had been: "Go to Nineveh with my message." Now that he has a second chance, God's word to him is still, "Go to Nineveh with my message."

This time Jonah obeys. He goes to Nineveh and proclaims that in forty days it will be *"overturned"* because of its sin (Jonah 3:4). They believe and repent, even the king. God spares the city, and Jonah tells God that's why he didn't want to come to Nineveh in the first place: he knew God was merciful and would forgive them if they responded to his message. Jonah would have preferred to have his nation's enemies judged (Jonah 4:1-2).

What I want you to notice is that Jonah's life got back on track when he obeyed the word God had given him— the same word God had given him before. A great revival took place through him, even if he didn't have a good attitude about it.

It works the same way for us. When we miss God's leading—by failing to do some basic thing all Christians should do, or by failing to follow his unique plan for our life—we get off track. At best, we stagnate. At worst, storms are unleashed to threaten us and those around us.

The only way to start making progress again is to do what we've already been told.

Have you missed God's leading in some basic Christian thing you should be doing? What do you need to do to get back on track?

_____

Have you missed God's leading in His unique plan for your life? What do you need to do to get back on track?

_____
_____

Chapter 8

BEING DELIVERED THROUGH PRAYER

FORREST MCCANNON WAS THE CHAIRMAN of deacons at the first church where I served as a fulltime pastor. He told me about the incident that brought him to the Lord.

He was crossing a river with other soldiers during World War II, somewhere in Europe, when the boat was hit by enemy fire and blew up. Forrest found himself in the water, yelling for help like the other men. Suddenly Jesus appeared to him, walking on the water. He said to Forrest, "Have no fear, I'm here." Forrest was rescued, and, in gratitude, he promised the Lord that he would live for Him from that moment on.

But when Forrest made it back to the states, he did not live for the Lord right away. It was some time before he gave his life to Jesus.

Forrest's story tells me a couple of things. The first thing it tells me is that God delights in rescuing people from trouble. That should not surprise us since one of Jesus' basic titles is Savior. The second thing Forrest's story tells me is that God delights in rescuing people not because the people deserve it, but because God is good. Forrest did not immediately keep his promise to God that he would live for Him. God knew he wouldn't, but delivered him anyway.

Praise the LORD, O my soul, and forget not all his benefits— who forgives all your sins and heals all your *diseases, **who redeems your life from the pit*** (Psalm 103:2-4a, emphasis added).

God delights in delivering people—in *forgiving* them, *healing* them, lifting them out of *pits*.

In verse 13 of the Model Prayer, Jesus told us to pray for deliverance:

But deliver us from the evil one (Matt. 6:13b).

Because we know that Jesus would not have told us to pray a prayer that didn't work, we can have faith that God will deliver us when we ask Him to. After all, He is the Savior; *saving* is what He does.

Let's consider three questions: **What will God deliver us from? Why will He do it? How will He do it?**

What will God deliver us from?

He will deliver us from daily troubles. That is, God will deliver us from the "small things." We have too much on our plate, and don't know how we're going to handle it all. An issue pops up at work, and we don't know the solution. There's an issue with the children, and we're not sure what to do. I've learned, in such situations, to just ask the Lord for help. Even when I don't know what to pray for, I just say, "Lord, please help me with this. I need you." And time after time He helps me—somehow things get better. I have found that the Lord loves doing this, and that kind of prayer has become a regular part of my life.

Are you stressed out? Don't know what to do about

some situation? Don't even know what to pray for exactly? How about just asking the Lord for help? He'll gladly step in.

The Lord will deliver us from daily troubles.

He will also deliver us from dangers. When the terrible earthquake hit Pakistan in the fall of 2005, our church helped with the relief effort through the Frontiers missionary group. Frontiers focuses on reaching Muslims with the Gospel, so they already had workers in the area ready to help. One of their converts to Christianity, a man they called "Graham" (his real name was withheld for his safety), arrived on the scene after the earthquake to help.

Graham heard a cry in the rubble. A little boy was trapped in heavy rocks and debris; only his head and one hand stuck out from the rubble. He was crying and begging for help. "Uncle, save me!" he called to Graham.

Graham pushed with all his might against a section of the wall that had collapsed on top of the boy, but it was far too heavy. He tried again and again but couldn't get it to budge. The boy continued screaming, and Graham saw that he was bleeding, but there was nothing he could do.

Then Graham sat down and told the boy to ask Jesus to help him, that Jesus was the only One strong enough. The boy asked him who Jesus was. Graham told him that Jesus was the Most Powerful Lord God.

The boy began asking Jesus to help him, calling out to him in the Pushtu dialect. Then Graham said, "When I say 'Jesus, you are our helper!' repeat this phrase with me. I will push the wall, but Jesus will move it."

They cried out together, "Jesus, you are our helper!" and with one push this one-and-a-half ton wall moved as if it were nothing! Graham pulled the boy to freedom, and said to him, "Your name is Emmanuel now. Your name means, 'God is with us.'"

The Lord will deliver us from daily troubles, and He will deliver us from serious dangers.

And He will deliver us spiritually. In other words, if we ask Him to, He will forgive our sins and save our souls. Romans 10:13 promises:

Everyone who calls on the name of the Lord will be saved.

This is the most important kind of deliverance.

I mentioned at the beginning of this book that I, a former atheist, met God through a simple heart-felt prayer. It was a prayer for salvation, though I didn't use those words exactly. I didn't know what to pray.

It happened when I was in my early twenties. Though I had been an atheist since high school, I had recently come to believe in the concept of God through a philosophy class taught by a Catholic ex-priest. He had convinced me, through an introduction to Aristotle's and Aquinas' thought, of the "reasonableness" of the idea of God. So I was open to the idea of God now, but I still did not have faith in Him.

I would like to say that from that point on I nobly sought out a relationship with God, but that's not the way it happened. What happened is I began to experience some difficulties in my life, so I decided I would try to read the Bible for some help—for some peace of mind. My mother had bought me a Bible, and I began to read a chapter of the New Testament each night. Sometimes what I read *did* make me feel better. However, sometimes what I read made me feel *worse*. That's because it was obvious that, if the words I was reading were true, I didn't measure up to God's standards—I was a "sinner." And sometimes I had trouble believing what I read, the miracles and so forth. But I kept reading.

One night, alone in my condominium, I decided it was time to make a decision. Was I willing to try to live the Christian life, as hard as it seemed? (This makes me smile now, because I have since then found that the Christian life is the most joyful life there is.) Was I willing to take a chance and ask God to take over my life? What if He wasn't there? Where would I turn next? But I decided I would go for it, and here's the prayer I prayed: "God, take over my mind."

I was in for the surprise of my life. A power—sort of like electricity and, somehow, sort of like water—hit me from the top of my head and flowed instantly through my whole body. It was the most powerful force I'd ever felt, but at the same time the gentlest—like an explosion of peace through my mind and body. It felt wonderful and scary all at once. I knew right away it was God. And I knew right away three things, three things that were written across my mind as if on banners: *There is a God. His name is Jesus. The Bible is His Word.*

I hopped out of bed—it was in the middle of the night—and went for a drive around the streets of Phoenix. I was totally happy, because I knew I'd just met God. But totally nervous, because I thought, *Uh oh. Now I know the truth. There's no excuse now.* I didn't realize I had just been saved, and had been forever accepted by God. I didn't know any theology yet.

From that moment on (it happened in 1983), my life changed. I haven't lived without trials since then, but

I've always had a joy and peace in my heart no matter what has been happening. I've never been able to get over the wonder of God's existence, the wonder that He revealed that existence to me, and the greatest wonder that He has forgiven me and saved me through faith in Jesus.

All in response to a prayer!

That can happen to you, too, if you've never accepted Jesus. Not in the same way necessarily; you and your circumstances are different, and God treats each one of us uniquely. But the results will be the same: forgiveness, peace, and an eternal relationship with God.

God will deliver us spiritually.

So we've seen *what* God will deliver us from—*daily troubles, dangers*, and *our sin*. The next question to consider is this:

Why does God deliver us?

We've already mentioned one reason He delivers us—*because of His goodness and love*. The Apostle John, who is generally considered to be the closest disciple to Jesus, wrote twice in the same chapter of the New Testament: *God is love* (1 John 4:8 and 1 John 4:16). God doesn't just *have* love. God *is* love. That means that everything He has ever done, is doing now, or ever will do is based on love. It's His nature. He can't act otherwise. (Even His acts of judgment, when properly understood, are based on love.) God delivers us because that's what love does.

The other reason God delivers us is *because it stirs our love for Him*. When you know that God has done something for you—something you needed, something you could not do for yourself (if you *could* have done it for yourself, you would not have needed to call on Him for deliverance)—you never forget it. It touches your heart. You know you were a recipient of God's love, and this stirs your love for God—as the Apostle John also wrote,

We love because he first loved us (1 John 4:19).

The Apostle Paul is an example of this. No apostle accomplished more for Christianity than Paul. Paul was the apostle primarily responsible for taking the Gospel to the Gentiles (the non-Jewish world), carrying it all the way to Rome, establishing churches as he went. In addition, he wrote about half the books of the New Testament. In fact, if you are a Christian today, it can very likely be traced back to the Apostle Paul's ministry. No apostle accomplished more for Christianity than Paul.

But then again no apostle had been forgiven as much as Paul, at least from a human perspective. The other apostles were "ordinary sinners," like the rest of us. Paul was an "ordinary sinner" and then some; he was the chief persecutor of the early church! He went around imprisoning people who believed in Jesus (Acts 8:3, 9:1-2), and he participated in the execution of the first Christian martyr (Acts 7:58). Paul was a sinner and then some—an active opponent of God. From a human perspective, no apostle had been forgiven as much as Paul.

It was the knowledge of this forgiveness—of God's great spiritual deliverance of him—that inspired Paul to live so fervently for the Lord, as he wrote:

For I am the least of the apostles and do not even deserve to be called an apostle, because I persecuted the church of God. But by the grace of God I am what I am, and his grace to me was not without effect. No, I worked harder than all of them—yet not I, but the grace of God that was with me (1 Cor. 15:9-10).

It was God's deliverance of Paul that stirred Paul's love for Him.

God delivers us because He loves us, and because He knows it inspires our love for Him.

We have seen *what* God will deliver us from, and *why* He will deliver us. The third question to consider:

How does God deliver us?

He delivers us in all kinds of ways, but I have found that there's usually some *surprise* element to it. The deliverance or solution usually comes in some way I am not expecting. I think God does that to remind me that the deliverance was from Him, not something I thought up. And also to remind me that He is sovereign, and can work things out in any way He wishes. And also, I think, to delight me—I love to see Him doing things in ways I didn't expect.

A Christian named Frederick Nolan was fleeing persecution in North Africa, his pursuers chasing him through the countryside. He ran and ran but couldn't shake them. Finally, exhausted, he fell into a cave, waiting for them to find him soon. But as he waited, he noticed a spider weaving a web at the mouth of the cave. Within minutes, the spider had spun an intricate web across the entrance to the cave. The pursuers arrived and approached the cave to look in it. But when they saw the web, they left! They apparently concluded *the man can't be in the cave. There's an unbroken web over the entrance.* Frederick Nolan later said, "Where God is, a spider's web is like a wall. Where God is not, a wall is like a spider's web."

When you ask God for deliverance, keep your eyes open. It will probably come in a way you didn't expect.

SUMMARY

God delights in rescuing people. Jesus promised in the Model Prayer that God would "deliver us from the evil one" if we asked. He will deliver us from daily troubles, from danger, and—most importantly—from our own sin. He delivers us because He loves us, and because His deliverance will inspire us to love Him. He delivers us in a variety of ways, but there's usually something surprising about the way it comes.

DIGGING DEEPER

Let's dig a little deeper now and see what some other Bible passages have to say about being delivered through prayer. We'll look at what the Scriptures say, then consider how it applies to our personal lives. There will be a place to record your answers; below that I will give my suggested answers.

If you prefer to continue reading specifically about the Model Prayer, you can turn to Chapter 9 now, and return here later to dig a little deeper.

THREE ENEMIES (FROM GALATIANS 5:1617,19-21; JAMES 4:4; 1 PETER 5:8)

Around 1980, a retired couple searched the globe for an out-of-the-way place to get away from it all, to spend their Golden Years in peace.

They picked the Falkland Islands, a group of islands off of the southern tip of South America—a remote place most people had never heard of. Shortly after their arrival, however, Argentina invaded the islands. It seems they disputed the United Kingdom's claim to them, a claim that stretches back to the days of England's empire. Well, the United Kingdom did not take kindly to the seizure of its property, never mind that the property was thousands of miles away, in another hemisphere, and toward the bottom of the world. They sent their own troops, ships, and planes to take it back. And thus began the Falkland Islands War, which lasted a couple of months, until Argentine forces surrendered in June 1982.

This retired couple, looking for a peaceful, out-of-the-way place in the world, found themselves in the middle of a war.

You can't get away from conflict in this world. Ever since the fall of the human being into sin, we have lived in the middle of a spiritual battlefield, a battlefield that often puts us in need of deliverance through prayer. That is why it is good to know that God has promised to "deliver us" us if we ask.

The Bible identifies three enemies that bring conflict into our life, and often cause us to need deliverance through prayer.

The first enemy is referred to as the "flesh."

But I say, walk by the Spirit, and you will not carry out the desire of the flesh. For the flesh sets its desire against the Spirit, and the Spirit against the flesh; for these are in opposition to one another (Gal. 5:16-17b, NASB).

Notice the *"flesh"* is "in opposition to" the Spirit. It is in opposition to God's work in our life. When the Bible refers to the flesh negatively like this, as our enemy, it is not to say that there is anything inherently wrong with our physical body—after all, God designed it for us. It is referring to the natural desires—housed in our physical body—that are often in conflict with God's will: lusts, passions, weaknesses, bad habits, and so on.

The Bible lists some examples of the sins of the flesh:

Now the deeds of the flesh are evident, which are: immorality, impurity, sensuality, idolatry, sorcery, enmities, strife, jealousy, outbursts of anger, disputes, dissensions, factions, envying, drunkenness, carousing, and things like these, of which I forewarn you, just as I have forewarned you, that those who practice such things will not inherit the kingdom of God (Gal. 5:19-21, NASB).

The flesh brings conflict into our life through our weakness to these various sins. When we give into them, they land us in various kinds of trouble.

For example, there was a foreman in a construction company who was always passed over for promotion. He was hardworking, knowledgeable, but he never got promoted. A younger employee asked him about this one

163

day, "Why don't they ever promote you? You're one of the best workers here."

"Well," the foreman said, "years ago I had an argument with the supervisor . . . and I won."

This foreman failed to advance because he gave into his temper one day. A sin of the flesh (see *"outbursts of anger,"* verse 20) landed him in trouble.

What sin of the flesh has landed you into the most trouble in your life?

_____

The second enemy that brings conflict into our life is the "world."

You adulterous people, don't you know that friendship with the world is hatred toward God? Anyone who chooses to be a friend of the world becomes an enemy of God (James 4:4).

The Bible says the *"world"* is not friendly to God's purposes, to God's will for our life. When the Bible refers to the world negatively like this, as our enemy, it is not referring to the people of the world. We know that God loves them, as Jesus said, *"For God so loved the world that he gave his one and only Son, that whoever believes in him shall not perish but have eternal life"* (John 3:16). The Bible is referring to the *ways* of the world, which so often tend to be in opposition to God's ways.

The main way the world brings conflict into our life is through the pressure to conform to its, and the crowd's, ways rather than to God's Word. It is hard to go against the flow.

Even Peter, the lead apostle, fell prey to the influence of the crowd. When Jesus was arrested the night before His crucifixion, Peter bravely followed Him to His first trial before the high priest. I believe Peter had every intention of standing by his Savior's side that night. He had earlier claimed that he would die for Jesus, and had pulled a sword to protect him when the soldiers came to arrest him. But that was before Peter felt the pressure of the crowd:

But when they had kindled a fire in the middle of the courtyard and had sat down together, Peter sat down with them (Luke 22:55).

Notice that "Peter sat down with them"—"them" being the disbelieving crowd. He took a seat with the group that was against Jesus.

Watch what happens next:

A servant girl saw him seated there in the firelight. She looked closely at him and said, "This man was with Him."

But he denied it. "Woman, I don't know Him," he said.

A little later someone else saw him and said, "You also are one of them." "Man, I am not!" Peter replied.

About an hour later another asserted, "Certainly this fellow was with Him, for he is a Galilean."

Peter replied, "Man, I don't know what you're talking about!" Just as he was speaking, the rooster crowed. The Lord turned and looked straight at Peter. Then Peter remembered the word the Lord had spoken to him: "Before the rooster crows today, you will disown me

three times."   And he went outside and wept bitterly
(Luke 22:56-62).

The pressure to conform to the crowd was too much
for Peter. He loved his Lord with all his heart, but found
himself denying Him in the hour of His greatest need. It
is hard indeed to go against the flow.

Christian author Max Lucado tells about the time he
had to catch an early flight. He was really tired and dozed
off while waiting for the plane. Suddenly he was roused
from his sleep by the noise of a crowd moving toward
the boarding ramp. He hurriedly gathered his belongings
and joined them. When he took his seat on the plane, he
slipped into another nap.

Some time later he awakened to the bright morning
sun shining through the window. He heard the flight
attendant announce their estimated time of arrival in
Houston. The problem was, he was supposed to be going
to Denver! Awakening in the terminal and seeing the
crowd boarding the plane, he had simply followed
along—and boarded the wrong plane.

It is hard to go against the flow. That's why the Bible
warns us in 1 Corinthians 15:33: *Do not be misled: "Bad
company corrupts good character."* That's why we need
to spend a healthy amount of time around other
Christians at church:

*Let us not give up meeting together, as some are in
the habit of doing, but let us encourage one another—
and all the more as you see the Day approaching* (Heb.
10:25).

Where are you feeling pressure to conform to the

world's ways?

_____

_____

The third enemy that brings conflict into our life is the devil.

Be self-controlled and alert. Your enemy the devil prowls around like a roaring lion looking for someone to devour (1 Pet. 5:8).

It is a mistake to put too much emphasis on the devil. He is only a fallen angel, served by other fallen angels, now called demons. He is nowhere near as powerful as God. He is not even as powerful as the least powerful holy angel. When Satan was evicted from heaven for rebelling against God, he lost all of his real power. It is a mistake to put too much emphasis on him.

It is also a mistake to be unaware of him. Two of the most devastating days in American history were the Japanese attack on Pearl Harbor on December 7, 1941, launching us into World War II, and the terrorist attacks on the World Trade Center and the Pentagon on September 11, 2001. Both of these attacks were the result of our nation being unaware of an enemy. Likewise, it is unwise for the Christian to be unaware our enemy Satan.

What do you think is the main way Satan attacks us and brings conflict into our life? When people think of Satan, the prince of evil, bringing spiritual warfare against them, they may imagine some special spiritual weapon or power he has to bring against them—like something out of a Hollywood movie. But in truth his greatest weapon can be as quiet as a whisper. The main way Satan attacks us is with a simple lie.

This is the weapon he brought against Adam and Eve in the first temptation. God had told them they would die if they ate the forbidden fruit (Gen. 2:17), but Satan said to them, *"You will not surely die . . . God knows that when you eat of it your eyes will be opened, and you will be like God, knowing good and evil"* (Gen. 3:4-5). He simply lied to them. They would in fact die as a result of eating the forbidden fruit, and they would not become like God—quite the opposite.

The lie is the weapon Satan uses to attack us. If we believe his lies, we fall for his temptations, and he gains power over our lives.

In 1996, a thirty-eight-year-old security guard at a Pennsylvania middle school convinced fourteen-year-old Tanya Kach to run away and live with him. To keep her with him, the security guard convinced Tanya that no one cared she was gone, and that her parents weren't looking for her. "You're stupid," he told her. "You're immature. Nobody cares about you but me." She stayed with him for ten years, not knowing any better.

Eventually, Tanya was allowed to take short trips away from the house while the man was at work. She became friends with the owner of local Deli Mart, who learned her real identity, and alerted the police.

Tanya was rescued and reunited with her family.

Tanya learned that she had been lied to all those years. In fact, her father had been desperately searching for her all along. He had posted her picture on thousands of flyers and milk cartons. Her father said, "It was exactly ten years, one month, and eleven days, and there wasn't a day that went by that I didn't think of her. I just say thank you, there is a God, and He brought my little girl back home." The security guard had controlled Tanya through a lie.

Satan works the same way against us. Using our own misguided thoughts, the words of other people, messages from our culture, and various other means, he tells us a lie: "God doesn't love you." "Doing those drugs won't hurt you." "You can't be forgiven." "Go ahead, you won't get caught." "God doesn't answer your prayers." If we believe his lies, we fall for his temptations, and he gains power over us. (That is why Jesus said, "Then you will know the truth, and the truth will set you free" (John 8:32).)

Can you think of any lies you've been tempted to believe?

_____

_____

Our three enemies bring conflict into our life—the flesh through our natural weaknesses, the world through the pressure to conform, and the devil through his lies. Because of this conflict, we often find ourselves in situations from which we need to be delivered. That is why it is good to know that God has promised to "deliver us" us if we ask.

He will even deliver us when the trouble we find ourselves in is of our own making—if we're in trouble because we've allowed ourselves to be defeated by one of our enemies. A friend of mine, several years after becoming a Christian, developed a substance abuse problem. He was cocaine and marijuana dependent. His addiction had grown so terrible that his wife left him. Finally, desperate for help, he checked himself into a rehab center in St. Paul, Minnesota.

An initial urinalysis collected upon check-in showed extreme levels of THC in his system. Cocaine will stay in a person's system for only a few days, but marijuana for over a month.

That night he fell to his knees on the cold tile of a hospital room and called on God to change his life. It seemed to him that an incredible light was present in that dark little hospital room, though when he opened his eyes the room was still dark. It seemed that he spent only a few minutes in prayer, but he realized later it must have been over half an hour.

God heard him. My friend's life was changed that night. His marriage was restored and he eventually went into youth work, then seminary, and finally the mission field.

But here's the amazing thing. The very next morning, according to standard protocol, another urinalysis was taken at the rehab center. A few hours later, they asked him for another urinalysis, then another, and finally one more—all in the span of ten hours. The reason? The tests showed no traces of the drugs that had been in his system the night before! They had never had a client go from extreme positive in THC levels to extreme negative the next morning. In fact, this was impossible. They figured there must be some mistake. Later in outpatient care he was even accused of faking the initial test, though all admitted they could see no reason why he would, or even how he could.

What happened? God heard my friend's heart cry for a new life. God heard his sincere prayer for change. And he instantly delivered him that night, even to the point of immediately and miraculously clearing the THC out of his system.

Of course, it doesn't always happen like that. Sometimes a person prays just as sincere a prayer and still has to struggle step by step toward freedom. But in this case Almighty God chose to deliver my friend immediately (though, he points out, it has taken his prayer life and walk with the Lord to continue to stay clean).

God will *"deliver us"* even when the trouble we are in is of our own making, even when we've allowed one of our enemies to defeat us. That is not to say that we can presume on His mercy, and expect Him to continue to deliver us if we continue to rebel against Him. God does expect us to get our lives straightened out. (More on that below in the "Making a Change" section.) But God is *"rich in mercy"* (Eph. 2:4), and is glad to rescue the person who calls on Him from a sincere heart. He is the Savior; saving is what He does.

THE REALITY OF SUPERNATURAL POWER

How would you define a miracle? Take a shot at it in the lines below:

_____

_____

_____

Theologians define a miracle as a supernatural intervention in the natural world—an act of God that interrupts or overrules natural laws. For example, naturally speaking, five loaves and two fish can only feed a small group of people. If a man takes those five loaves and two fish, breaks them, and hands out enough to feed thousands, there has been a supernatural intervention in the natural world. That is a miracle.

Some people don't believe in miracles. Atheists and agnostics may not believe in supernatural power at all. They may only admit the reality of the natural physical world. Even some Christians don't believe miracles are for today. They believe they were limited to Biblical times, and that they are not necessary today.

But the Model Prayer that Jesus taught us to pray presupposes the reality of miracles—the reality of a God who is willing to intervene in this world and help us. What's the point of praying, *"Give us today our daily bread," "lead us,"* or *"deliver us from the evil one"* if we don't believe that God will intervene on our behalf? We would be praying a prayer that didn't *work.* Jesus would not have taught us to do this. The Model Prayer presupposes a God who is willing to use His supernatural power on people's behalf.

And He is still willing to use it. In 1996, two pickup trucks collided on Brown Road in Mesa, Arizona. The driver of the truck at fault was instantly killed. The driver of the other truck was trapped in the cab of his truck— with flames quickly spreading from the engine area toward the cab.

Two brothers, air conditioning workers David and Kevin Estepp, were barbecuing in their nearby yard when they saw the fireball from the accident. They rushed to help. But the door of the pickup truck had gotten jammed in the wreck, and they couldn't get the driver out. They had to step back because of the smoke.

The *Arizona Republic* quoted David Estepp: "I remember hearing,

'Step back, get away, it's going to blow up,' from other bystanders. But it's like, you know, he's alive . . .

you couldn't just do nothing."

So the brothers stepped through the smoke, grabbed the steel doorframe, and pulled one more time. Somehow the steel began to bend . . . and bend . . . and bend. They bent it downward almost forty-five degrees, and pulled the trapped man free—less than a minute before the flames spread and engulfed the cab.

David Estepp didn't know how to explain how he and his brother bent that steel, but he said, "It was no brute strength, I tell you." Colin Williams, the Fire Department spokesman, said, "Some of the guys can't believe how it was done. It seemed like supernatural powers."

It seems like it to me, too. God is still willing to use his supernatural power on people's behalf. We can trust Him to help us when we call on Him to "deliver us."

Can you describe a time when you believe God's supernatural power delivered you?

_____

_____

_____

MAKING A CHANGE (FROM PROVERBS 29:1)

There's a saying, "An ounce of obedience is worth a pound of prayer." The point is that obeying God in the first place will save us from a lot of trouble, and make unnecessary a lot of desperate praying for deliverance from those troubles.

Obedience is not only the way to *avoid* trouble. It is often the only way *out* of trouble as well. As I mentioned in the "Three Enemies" section above, God is merciful and will often "deliver us" from problems that we ourselves have caused. But He will only answer these prayers for deliverance from self-made problems to a point. If we continue in the rebellious behavior that is causing the problems, we can expect His deliverance to end. The Bible says:

A man who remains stiff-necked after many rebukes will suddenly be destroyed—without remedy (Prov. 29: 1).

It is dangerous to assume that God will continue to deliver us from self-made problems. There comes a time when we have to make a change, or deliverance isn't coming.

A few summers ago we had a gnat problem in our house. It started gradually—one here, a few there—but before long it was an invasion. They flew throughout the house: the kitchen, bathrooms, and the study. They landed in our food, swam in our glasses, drowned in the water around our sinks.

I killed scores of them, thinking that eventually I'd get rid of them.

After all, how many of them could keep slipping in through the screen door or vents or by way of the dog's fur? But I made no headway; their number kept increasing.

Finally, we began to suspect that all of these gnats couldn't be slipping in from outside. My wife examined a houseplant she had received in the mail, and it was infested. The gnats had apparently come into the house by way of this plant, and then spread to other household plants. It was an inside job! She took the plants outside, and the gnat problem was solved overnight.

We would never have gotten rid of the gnats if we had

not gotten rid of their breeding ground—the houseplants. I could have gone around swatting them and complaining about them the rest of my life. We had to deal with their source.

Likewise, there's a point where nothing will get rid of our problems until we deal with the source. Until we make a change in our behavior. God may have delivered us once or twice from the problems that have arisen from our rebellious or unwise ways, but this time He is waiting on a change.

Is there a problem in your life that is not responding to prayer? What needs to be changed?

_____

_____

_____

"An ounce of obedience is worth a pound of prayer."

Chapter 9

KEEPING ON TRACK THROUGH PRAYER

PARADE MAGAZINE HOSTED A PHOTO contest a few years ago, asking people to send in photographs of interesting road signs in America.

Among the top ten were the following signs:

- A sign in the Mojave Desert that said: "Absolutely Nothing–Next 22 Miles."
- A sign near Tallahassee, Florida, with this helpful insight: "Water on Road When Raining."
- A stop sign in Shreveport, Louisiana, with the official subtitle: "And Smell the Roses."
- A sign in central Oregon: "Soft Shoulder—Blind Curves—Steep Grade—Big Trucks—Good Luck!"
- And a sign next to a traffic light in Fort Walton Beach, Florida: "This Light Never Turns Green."

These are interesting road signs, to be sure, but perhaps not all that helpful. As we travel the road of life, we also encounter many "signs" along the way, messages from peers and culture and media telling us which way to go and how to live. They are often very interesting messages, but many of them are not very helpful. Many of them are even destructive.

As we come to the end of the Model Prayer, we find some "road signs" for life that we can trust. Jesus told us to end our prayer with this statement:

For yours is the kingdom and the power and the glory forever. Amen (Matt. 6:13c).*

Why did Jesus tell us to end our prayer with this statement? Because it contains *three truths we should have in the forefront of our mind as we get up from prayer* and head back out into the world—truths that will serve as "road signs" to keep us on track through life.

We've been studying the Model Prayer with the understanding that Jesus would not have told us to pray a prayer that didn't work. We're adjusting our focus a bit as we look at this last statement of the prayer. Just as Jesus would not have told us to pray a prayer that didn't work, He also would not have told us to pray a prayer that *didn't matter.* He told us to end our prayer with the statement *"yours is the kingdom and the power and the glory"* because it contains three truths we should have in mind as we get up from prayer.

Let's look at what these truths are, and how they will keep us on track through life.

TRUTH #1: GOD IS IN CHARGE.

Jesus told us to pray, *"Yours is the kingdom."* When we get up from prayer, we're to keep in mind that the "kingdom" belongs to God. He's the One in charge.

A pastor who was an avid golfer was taking part in a local golf tournament. As he prepared to tee off, storm clouds rolled in. The organizer of the tournament pointed them out to the pastor, and said with a smile, "Preacher, I trust you'll see to it that the weather won't turn bad on us." The pastor shook his head and said, "Sorry. I'm in sales, not management!"

It is important that we get up from prayer remembering that God is in charge. As we can see, it will relieve us of unnecessary burdens. It is not up to us to control the weather, the world, or even all the circumstances of our life. God is ultimately in charge. It relieves us of burdens and helps us enjoy life when we remember this.

Let's talk about what it means that God is in charge, examine some evidence that God is in charge, and then explore the benefits of knowing that God is in charge.

What does it mean that God is in charge?

It does not mean that everything that happens is His will. That should be obvious since the Bible says, *All have sinned and fall short of the glory of God* (Rom. 3:23), and sin by its very definition is something that is against God's will. In addition, Jesus said, *"The thief comes only to steal and kill and destroy; I have come that they may have life, and have it to the full"* (John 10:10). So the *"thief"* (Satan) is doing many things against God's will in people's lives. Not everything that happens is God's will.

What does it mean, then, to say that God is in charge? It means that in spite of the rebellion and evil in the world, God is working out a plan. He will have the last word.

And it's a plan that will work out well for those who love God:

And we know that God causes all things to work together for good to those who love God, to those who are called according to his purpose (Rom. 8:28, NASB).

God is working out a plan, a plan that will turn out well for those who love Him. He will have the last word. That is what it means that God is in charge.

Is there any evidence that God is in charge in this crazy world?

There is plenty of evidence in history that God is charge, directing the world toward a good end. One example of God's hand at work in history can be seen in the circumstances that were in place when Christianity burst on the world scene, circumstances that worked together to give the new Christian message maximum impact. Four helpful circumstances were in place when Christianity was born:

1. The *Pax Romana*, or the Roman peace. Because of Rome's dominance, there was relative peace in the world in those days, at least as far as the influence of the Roman Empire stretched. Other nations did not dare challenge them. This meant that Christian missionaries could take the Gospel from nation to nation in relative safety.

2. The Roman road system. The Romans built some 50,000 miles of hard-surfaced roads, stretching as far away as Britain. They built them for military purposes. Christian missionaries used them to take the Gospel from nation to nation.

3. The prevalence of the Greek language. Greek was much like English is today, a sort of "universal" language among the nations of the Roman Empire, the common tongue. This gave the early Christians a language to share the Good News in as they traveled about. Even the New Testament was written in Greek.

4. The Dispersion, or Diaspora, of the Jewish people. Because of wars and exiles throughout their history, Jews had been forced from their homeland, and lived in cities throughout the Roman Empire. This meant that they established synagogues in these cities where they worshiped God and taught the Old Testament, including the promises of a coming Messiah. Not only Jews came to the synagogue, but "God-fearers"—Gentiles who worshiped the God of the Jews—also attended. All of this made for a ready audience, among Jews and non-Jews, when the apostles arrived with the Gospel.

These four helpful circumstances were present on the world stage when Christianity was born, and enabled early believers to spread the faith with maximum impact. It was not an accident that they were present; it did not "just happen." God was in charge, directing world affairs.

Is there more evidence from history that God is in charge? Well, in 1998, *Life Books* published *The Life Millennium: The 100 Most Important Events and People of the Past 1,000 Years*, in which it ranked the most important events since the year 1,000. Making the list were events such as the Wright brothers' flight at Kitty Hawk (#27), the dropping of the atomic bombs on Japan to end World War II (#16), and Columbus's voyage to the New World (#2).

But the event ranked #1—the most important event of the last millennium, according to *Life*—was the printing of the Bible on Gutenberg's printing press in 1455. Why is this event ranked #1? This event led to the Bible, as well as other books, being distributed to the public at large for the first time. All of which led, eventually, to the Renaissance, the Protestant Reformation, and the subsequent political and industrial revolutions—which brought us, among other things, the United States of America.

But the point I want to make is that the invention of the printing press at this time in history was no accident. It happened about the same time scholars were starting to translate the Bible out of archaic Latin into the languages of the people. John Wycliffe had already created an English translation (about 1382). William Tyndale was about to follow suit (in 1524), for which he'd be burned at the stake. And Martin Luther— hiding from his enemies in a lonely castle and growing a big beard as a disguise—was about to produce one in the German language (1522). It was at this moment in history that the printing press was invented.

Was this a coincidence? I don't believe so. I believe God was in charge, directing history.

Let me share one more example of God's hand at work in history directing world events. Have you ever considered how fortunate it was that America developed the atomic bomb during World War II and not Nazi Germany? Especially when you consider that Albert Einstein, whose theories led to the creation of the bomb, was a German, and lived in Germany as Hitler came to power? It would have been more likely, it seems, for Germany to have ended up with the bomb.

But Einstein was a Jew, and Hitler hated Jews. When Hitler began to persecute them, Einstein fled to America. When World War II broke out, he wrote one of the most important letters in history. He wrote to President Roosevelt, warning that the Germans might be working on the development of an atomic bomb, and urging "watchfulness and, if necessary, quick action on the part of" the United States. This letter led to the Manhattan Project, and to the United States developing the atomic bomb and not the Nazis. (You can read Einstein's letter for yourself on the Internet.)

Was it just luck that the Free World developed the atomic bomb and not the Nazis? I don't think so. I believe God was in charge, directing world events. History reveals His hand at work.

We have seen what it means that God is in charge—that He is working out a plan, a plan that will turn out well for those who love Him. He will have the last word.

We have seen evidence that God is in charge in history.

What is the benefit of knowing that God is in charge?

The benefit of knowing that God is in charge is peace of mind. When we get up from prayer knowing that His *"is the kingdom"*—that He is in charge of the world, and of my life in it—we can have peace of mind as we go about our day.

We sorely need this peace of mind today. The National Institute of Mental Health recently stated that anxiety disorders are the number one mental health problem in the U. S., afflicting some 19 million adults. Anxiety is also the number one mental health problem for children ages nine to seventeen. We have a need for peace of mind today.

Are you stressed out? A couple of psychiatrists, Thomas Holmes and Richard Rahe, developed a list of Life's Most Stressful Events. Take a look at the list and see if you're dealing with any of these stress-inducers:

• Death of a Spouse

- Divorce
- Marital Separation
- Imprisonment
- Death of a Close Family Member
- Personal Injury or Illness
- Marriage
- Dismissal from Work
- Marital Reconciliation
- Retirement

Are you dealing with any of these stress-inducers? Other events on the Holmes and Rahe Stress Scale include pregnancy, a change in financial status, a major mortgage, a child leaving home, a change in residence, and even a change in church activities.

Peace of mind can be hard to come by.

The key to having peace of mind is believing that God is in charge— of the world, and of my life in it.

I read about a woman who always left behind little crumpled-up pieces of paper when she left church. The man who cleaned up after services would find them in the pew where she sat. Little notes were written on the pieces of paper: "Debbie—illness," "Mike—a job," and "Rent money."

The man took the notes to the pastor and told him about it. The pastor asked the lady about it the next Sunday, and she explained, "I know you'll think it's silly, Pastor, but I saw a sign on a city bus that said, 'Take your worries to church and leave them there.' I write my worries down on those little pieces of paper every Sunday morning. When the service is over, I crumple them up and leave them in the pew. I think God wants me to leave my problems at church."

This woman had found the key to peace of mind:

believing that God was in charge of her life. She was doing what the Bible tells us to do:

Cast all your anxiety on Him because He cares for you (1 Pet. 5:7).

You can do it, too. You can give Him your worries and trust Him to be in charge of them.

The benefit of knowing that God is in charge is peace of mind.

The first truth we should have in mind as we get up from prayer is *"yours is the kingdom."* We should know that God is in charge.

What part of your life do you need to believe God is in charge of, in order to have peace of mind?

_____

_____

TRUTH #2: GOD HAS THE POWER I NEED.

Jesus also told us to pray, *"Yours is . . . the power."* When we get up from prayer, we're to keep in mind that God has all the power we're going to need for that day.

The Bible has always declared that God is all-powerful—He is identified as the "Almighty" some 342 times in its pages (the New International Version). The Bible describes Him making the world without lifting a finger, but just speaking it into existence. The Bible describes His many miracles, from the parting of the Red Sea to healing the sick to raising the dead. The Bible has always declared His power.

But lately the evidence of God's power has been coming from a new source: modern science. Lately, scientists have found evidence of an "Anthropic Principle" in the world. Anthropic is a big word that simply means related to man. The Anthropic Principle refers to the growing body of evidence that suggests that our world was purposely designed as a home for humans.

You see, the universe as a whole is a very inhospitable place—a very dangerous neighborhood. As far as we know, there's no other place in it that can support human life except our little corner of it, this little dot of a planet called earth. But here—against great odds—a number of conditions have combined to make life possible. These conditions are called "Anthropic Constants."

Scientists have so far discovered at least 122 "Anthropic Constants." Here are just a few of them:

- The earth had to be just the right distance away from the sun, about 93 million miles. Much closer and it would be too hot. Much farther away and it would be too cold. Our planet happens to be just the right distance away from its star.

- The earth had to rotate at just the right speed, in twenty-four hours. If the rotation took longer, temperature differences between night and day would be too drastic. If the rotation took less time, atmospheric wind velocities would be too great.

- Earth had to have just the right amount of oxygen, twentyone percent of the atmosphere. If it were twenty-five percent, fires would break out spontaneously. If it were fifteen percent, people would suffocate.

- Even Jupiter plays a role in our survival. Because of its position in its orbit around the sun, its gravitational field sucks away asteroids and comets that could strike the earth.

These are just a few conditions that had to come together in our little corner of the universe to make human life possible. There are many more. What are the odds all this happened by accident?

Norman L. Geisler and Frank Turek, in their wonderful book *I Don't Have Enough Faith to Be an Atheist*, tell the story of astrophysicist Hugh Ross, who sat down to calculate the probability that all of these conditions—the 122 "Anthropic Constants" scientists have discovered so far—could occur by accident for any planet in the universe. Assuming that the number of planets in the universe is 10^{22} power (that's a one with twenty-two zeros after it), Ross said there's just one chance in 10^{138} power (that's a one with 138 zeros after it) that all these constants happened by accident for planet earth. That's a stunningly high number: that number is higher than the number of atoms in the universe! (There are "only" 10^{70} power atoms in the universe.)

Think about that. Everything is made up of atoms; an atom is a million times smaller than the thickness of a human hair; the smallest speck that can be seen under a regular microscope contains more than 10 billion atoms. Imagine how many there must be in the universe. But this astrophysicist says there's just one chance in a number greater than the number of atoms in the universe that all the constants necessary for life came together by accident for earth.

No wonder Geisler and Turek entitled their book *I Don't Have Enough Faith to Be an Atheist*. The evidence for an all-powerful Designer is overwhelming.

If God has the power to orchestrate the cosmic forces

of the universe, and against all odds make a home for us here on earth, then certainly He has all the power we need to help us through our day.

Are you relying on His power? One New Year's Day, in the Tournament of Roses parade, a beautiful float suddenly sputtered and quit—it was out of gas. The whole parade was held up until someone could run and get a can of gas. Who was the sponsor of this float? The Standard Oil Company! This float, representing one of the biggest gasoline producers in the world, was out of gas.

That is a picture of us all too often. All of God's power is available to us, but we're not relying on it.

King David learned to rely on God's power. His daily prayer time included a practice that reminded him of the power of God:

*In the morning, O LORD, you hear my voice; in the morning I lay my requests before you and **wait in expectation*** (Ps. 5:3, emphasis added).

David's practice was to lay his requests before the Lord in the morning, and then "wait in expectation" to see what God was going to do. This practice kept David relying on God's power day to day.

The second truth we should have in mind as we get up from prayer is "yours is . . . the power." We should trust that God has all the power we're going to need that day.

What can you do to remind yourself that God has all the power you're going to need that day?

_____

_____

TRUTH #3: MY GOAL IN LIFE IS TO GLORIFY GOD.

The last thing Jesus told us to pray when we get up from prayer is, *"yours is . . . the glory."* When we get up from prayer and head out into the world, we're to keep in mind that our goal in life is to glorify God.

What does it mean to glorify God? It means to live in a way that honors Him. Jesus referred to this when he said, *"Let your light so shine before men, that they may see your good works and glorify your Father in heaven"* (Matt. 5:16, NKJV).

If our goal in life is to glorify God, it will have some practical results. Let's look at them.

First, if my goal in life is to glorify God, I will want to do the right thing— and this will simplify my life and keep me out of a lot of trouble.

You may have heard about the man who, in September of 2003, decided to ship himself from New York City to Dallas—in a wooden crate! He somehow packed himself in the crate. The crate journeyed by truck, plane, and delivery van—until it finally arrived at his parents' house. Then he began to break out of the box. When the authorities caught up to him, he explained that he was homesick. He thought it would be cheaper to get home by crate, rather than buy a ticket like everybody else.

What did he get for his troubles? A fine of $1,500 and 120 days of house arrest. At the cost of the fine, he could have purchased four roundtrip tickets to see his parents.

How much simpler, and cheaper, it would have been to do the right thing in the first place.

When we fail to do the right thing, we complicate our life. The speeding ticket raises our insurance rates, or costs us a day in traffic school. The unkind comment leads to a strained relationship. The lapse at work causes a mess of trouble. Sin complicates things.

On the other hand, if our goal in life is to glorify God, we will want to do the right thing. This will simplify our life and keep us out of a lot of trouble.

Second, if my goal in life is to glorify God, I will get my needs met.

Jesus said that living to please God has a very practical result: *"But seek first His kingdom and His righteousness, and all these things will be given to you as well"* (Matt. 6:33). The practical result of living to please God is having *"all these things"* given to us. The *"things"* He is talking about in that passage are material things: food, clothes, and drink (Matt. 6:25-34). Living to please God will get our needs met.

Our church was located near Luke Air Force Base. A number of airmen and women worshiped with us over the years. I noticed something about them. They never worried about where their next meal was coming from. They never worried if they'd have anything to wear to work that week (uniforms are supplied). They never worried about getting the training and equipment they needed to do their jobs. If they got sick, there was the base hospital. When they retire, there will be benefits. They weren't rich, but these servicemen and women had their needs met. Because they'd committed to serve the

U.S. Air Force, the U.S. Air Force had committed to take care of them. Civilians—well, we're on our own.

This is the way it works with God, too, according to Jesus. If we are living to please Him, He will see to it that we are taken care of—"all these things will be given to" us. The second practical result of living to glorify is getting our needs met.

Third, if my goal in life is to glorify God, it will result in a close relationship with Him.

The Bible says that God looks at our motivation: *"All a man's ways seem innocent to him, but motives are weighed by the LORD"* (Prov. 16:2). When God looks at our motivation and sees that it is to please Him, it touches his Heart—and He draws close to us.

I once preached a series of services at a church made up of people who had migrated to Phoenix from the nation of India. Over the course of the weekend I learned that the pastor's marriage had been arranged, and that this is a common practice among Christians in India. I asked the pastor's wife, Sucheta, about it.

She told me that when a man comes to ask for a Christian girl's hand, the girl has a question she asks—a question Sucheta herself asked the pastor. If the man gives the correct answer, the marriage is on. If not, the girl opposes the marriage.

The question the girl asks: "Do you want a dowry?" A dowry, of course, is a gift of goods or money that the bride's family gives the groom for the trouble of taking this female off their hands. If the man answers, "Yes, I require a dowry"—*bzzzzzz,* wrong answer! No marriage. If he says, "No, I only want the girl"—*ding, ding, ding,* right answer! The girl agrees to the marriage.

Why this question? The marriage may be arranged, but the girl wants to know the man's motivation. Does he want her for herself, or for some gift or money he's going to receive?

In the same way, God looks at our motivation. If it is to bring Him glory—to please Him above all else—He draws close to us. Can there be anything more important than that?

SUMMARY

As we travel the road of life, we receive many conflicting messages about which way we should go and how we should live. But at the end of the Model Prayer Jesus gives us three "road signs" for life that we can trust—three truths that will keep us on track as we get up from prayer and head out into the world. Truth #1: God is in charge (*"Yours is the kingdom"*). Truth #2: God has the power I need (*"Yours is . . . the power"*). Truth #3: My goal in life is to glorify God (*"Yours is . . . the glory forever"*).

Which one of the three "road signs" do you need to focus on the most at this time in your life?

_____

* In some Bible translations, you will find this last statement of the Model Prayer, "for yours is the kingdom and the power and the glory forever. Amen," in the margin or in brackets, perhaps with a note explaining that the translators set it apart from the rest of the text because it's not found in the earliest New Testament manuscripts. The translators and publishers are not necessarily saying

that this statement should not be considered a part of the Word of God; they are simply being honest with their scholarship. There's no reason for anything but openness and honesty when it comes to New Testament scholarship, because it is the most verified ancient document in history, with more surviving copies than other ancient works, and copies closer in years to the originals than other ancient works, and copies that agree in all the principles—with only minor variations here and there among the manuscripts. When it comes to this last line of the Model Prayer, the church throughout history has generally recognized it as containing the actual words of Jesus. I do, too.

Chapter 10

THE MODEL PRAYER AS A PRAYER GUIDE

WE HAVE LEARNED THAT PRAYING the Model Prayer should not be an empty ritual, in which the words are repeated over and over again in an effort to earn God's favor. Jesus said this in His introduction to the Model Prayer:

"And when you pray, do not keep on babbling like pagans, for they think they will be heard because of their many words" (Matt. 6:7).

The Model Prayer was given as a guide to prayer—to show us *what* to pray about, and *how* to pray about it.

One way we can use the Model Prayer as a guide is by letting it serve as a framework for our prayer. What I mean is, we don't pray the lines of the prayer mindlessly over and over again; rather, we pray one line of the prayer thoughtfully, and allow it to be a springboard to more prayer along that topic. Then we move on to another line of the prayer.

Let me show you what I mean.

First, find a private meeting place with God, obeying Jesus' instructions in His introduction to the prayer:

- *"But when you pray, go into your room, close the door and pray to your Father, who is unseen. Then your Father, who sees what is done in secret, will reward you"* (Matt. 6:6).

Go to your private meeting place, knowing that Almighty God Himself notices and responds—He will reward you for it!

Then begin to pray the individual lines of the prayer, using them as introductions to more conversation with God about that topic:

- *"Our Father in heaven, hallowed be your name"* (Matt. 6:9).

Pray this line, then spend more time worshiping God as your heart feels led. Thank Him for being your Father, loving you, and taking care of you. Acknowledge His holiness. Praise Him for His beauty and awesome power.

- *"Your kingdom come, your will be done on earth as it is in heaven"* (Matt. 6:10).

Spend time asking God to bring the power of His kingdom to earth—to change things that need changing.

- *"Give us today our daily bread"* (Matt. 6:11).

What needs do you have? Ask Him to meet them.

- *"Forgive us our debts"* (Matt. 6:12).

Confess your sins to Him, and accept His forgiveness—see 1 John 1:9.

- *"As we also have forgiven our debtors"* (Matt.

6:12).

In prayer, forgive those who have hurt you. Pray for them, and let it go!

- *"And lead us not into temptation"* (Matt. 6:13).

Do you need guidance in some situation? Ask God for it.

- *"But deliver us from the evil one"* (Matt. 6:13).

Ask God to give you victory in the troubles you're facing.

- *"For yours is the kingdom and the power and the glory forever. Amen"* (Matt. 6:13).

Get up from prayer with more praise in your heart.

As you enter the world again, keep in mind the truths of God's kingdom (He is in charge), power (He has all the power you need), and glory (He is the One you should live to please).

If you use the Model Prayer as a Prayer Guide like this, you will likely find:

First, it will help you concentrate. A wandering mind is one of the biggest obstacles to prayer. Using the Model Prayer as a framework for your prayer time will help you stay focused.

Second, you will probably have a hard time getting through the whole prayer! Jesus' words are anointed. As you let them guide you, you will probably find your heart overflowing with inspired prayer.

But who says you have to "get through" the prayer? When you come to prayer again, just pick up where you left off. Or, better yet, take the prayer with you in your heart throughout the day and *"pray without ceasing"* (1 Thess. 5:17, KJV).

Third, your prayer life will be well-rounded. Left to ourselves, we can get in a prayer rut, praying about and focusing on the same things. Praying the lines of the Model Prayer, focusing on their various topics, will stretch us.

Chapter 11

THE GREAT INVITATION

EMILY POST, THE ETIQUETTE EXPERT, was once asked, "What is the correct procedure if one receives an invitation from the White House, but has a previous engagement?" She responded, "An invitation to the White House . . . automatically cancels all other engagements."

If this is true of an invitation to the highest office in the land, how much more so of an invitation to the highest office in the universe—to talk to Almighty God Himself! We have all received this invitation, as the Bible declares: *"Let us then approach the throne of grace with confidence, so that we may receive mercy and find grace to help us in our time of need"* (Heb. 4:16). We are invited to the very "throne" of the universe through prayer.

- The throne is the place where things are decided.
- The throne is the place where we see things from heaven's point of view.
- The throne is the place where our Heavenly Father waits to receive us.

Prayer is indeed the Great Invitation. Do you have anything more important, or exciting, to do? You have received the invitation. RSVP today.

DEAR READER!

Thanks for reading my book. Please consider jotting a short review on Amazon. It would be much appreciated. Also, feel free to email me with comments or questions at billray@joyinthedesert.com

ABOUT THE AUTHOR

Once a devout atheist, William Ray became a Christian through a personal experience with Jesus at the age of 23, serving for more than two decades in pastoral ministry before pursuing the writing projects that had been placed on his heart. He holds the Master of Divinity degree from Southwestern Baptist Theological Seminary and an English degree from Grand Canyon University.

In addition to *Answered Prayer: The Jesus Plan*, William is the author of *Burden Stone: A Novel of the Camino De Santiago* and the science fiction series *The Lost Colony*. You may email him with comments or questions at billray@joyinthedesert.com

Made in United States
Troutdale, OR
01/25/2024

17143407R10116